1–2 SAMUEL

A 12-WEEK STUDY

Ryan Kelly

:: CROSSWAY®

WHEATON, ILLINOIS

Knowing the Bible: 1–2 Samuel, A 12-Week Study

Copyright © 2018 by Crossway

Published by Crossway
        1300 Crescent Street
        Wheaton, Illinois 60187

Cover design: Simplicated Studio

First printing 2018

Printed in the United States of America

Trade paperback ISBN: 978-1-4335-5374-5
EPub ISBN: 978-1-4335-5377-6
PDF ISBN: 978-1-4335-5375-2
Mobipocket ISBN: 978-1-4335-5376-9

Crossway is a publishing ministry of Good News Publishers.

VP		31	30	29	28	27	26	25	24	23
16	15	14	13	12	11	10	9	8	7	6	5

"This series is a tremendous resource for those wanting to study and teach the Bible with an understanding of how the gospel is woven throughout Scripture. Here are gospel-minded pastors and scholars doing gospel business from all the Scriptures. This is a biblical and theological feast preparing God's people to apply the entire Bible to all of life with heart and mind wholly committed to Christ's priorities."

BRYAN CHAPELL, President Emeritus, Covenant Theological Seminary; Senior Pastor, Grace Presbyterian Church, Peoria, Illinois

"Mark Twain may have smiled when he wrote to a friend, 'I didn't have time to write you a short letter, so I wrote you a long letter.' But the truth of Twain's remark remains serious and universal, because well-reasoned, compact writing requires extra time and extra hard work. And this is what we have in the Crossway Bible study series *Knowing the Bible*. The skilled authors and notable editors provide the contours of each book of the Bible as well as the grand theological themes that bind them together as one Book. Here, in a 12-week format, are carefully wrought studies that will ignite the mind and the heart."

R. KENT HUGHES, Visiting Professor of Practical Theology, Westminster Theological Seminary

"*Knowing the Bible* brings together a gifted team of Bible teachers to produce a high-quality series of study guides. The coordinated focus of these materials is unique: biblical content, provocative questions, systematic theology, practical application, and the gospel story of God's grace presented all the way through Scripture."

PHILIP G. RYKEN, President, Wheaton College

"These *Knowing the Bible* volumes provide a significant and very welcome variation on the general run of inductive Bible studies. This series provides substantial instruction, as well as teaching through the very questions that are asked. *Knowing the Bible* then goes even further by showing how any given text links with the gospel, the whole Bible, and the formation of theology. I heartily endorse this orientation of individual books to the whole Bible and the gospel, and I applaud the demonstration that sound theology was not something invented later by Christians, but is right there in the pages of Scripture."

GRAEME L. GOLDSWORTHY, former lecturer, Moore Theological College; author, *According to Plan, Gospel and Kingdom, The Gospel in Revelation*, and *Gospel and Wisdom*

"What a gift to earnest, Bible-loving, Bible-searching believers! The organization and structure of the Bible study format presented through the *Knowing the Bible* series is so well conceived. Students of the Word are led to understand the content of passages through perceptive, guided questions, and they are given rich insights and application all along the way in the brief but illuminating sections that conclude each study. What potential growth in depth and breadth of understanding these studies offer! One can only pray that vast numbers of believers will discover more of God and the beauty of his Word through these rich studies."

BRUCE A. WARE, Professor of Christian Theology, The Southern Baptist Theological Seminary

KNOWING THE BIBLE

J. I. Packer, Theological Editor
Dane C. Ortlund, Series Editor
Lane T. Dennis, Executive Editor

• • • • • •

Genesis	Psalms	Jonah, Micah, and Nahum	Ephesians
Exodus	Proverbs		Philippians
Leviticus	Ecclesiastes	Haggai, Zechariah, and Malachi	Colossians and Philemon
Numbers	Song of Solomon		
Deuteronomy	Isaiah	Matthew	1–2 Thessalonians
Joshua	Jeremiah	Mark	1–2 Timothy and Titus
Judges	Lamentations, Habakkuk, and Zephaniah	Luke	
Ruth and Esther		John	
1–2 Samuel	Ezekiel	Acts	Hebrews
1–2 Kings	Daniel	Romans	James
1–2 Chronicles	Hosea	1 Corinthians	1–2 Peter and Jude
Ezra and Nehemiah	Joel, Amos, and Obadiah	2 Corinthians	1–3 John
Job		Galatians	Revelation

• • • • • •

J. I. PACKER was the former Board of Governors' Professor of Theology at Regent College (Vancouver, BC). Dr. Packer earned his DPhil at the University of Oxford. He is known and loved worldwide as the author of the best-selling book *Knowing God*, as well as many other titles on theology and the Christian life. He served as the General Editor of the ESV Bible and as the Theological Editor for the *ESV Study Bible*.

LANE T. DENNIS is CEO of Crossway, a not-for-profit publishing ministry. Dr. Dennis earned his PhD from Northwestern University. He is Chair of the ESV Bible Translation Oversight Committee and Executive Editor of the *ESV Study Bible*.

DANE C. ORTLUND (PhD, Wheaton College) serves as senior pastor of Naperville Presbyterian Church in Naperville, Illinois. He is an editor for the Knowing the Bible series and the Short Studies in Biblical Theology series, and is the author of several books, including *Gentle and Lowly: The Heart of Christ for Sinners and Sufferers*.

TABLE OF CONTENTS

▲

SERIES PREFACE

KNOWING THE BIBLE, as the series title indicates, was created to help readers know and understand the meaning, the message, and the God of the Bible. Each volume in the series consists of 12 units that progressively take the reader through a clear, concise study of one or more books of the Bible. In this way, any given volume can fruitfully be used in a 12-week format either in group study, such as in a church-based context, or in individual study. Of course, these 12 studies could be completed in fewer or more than 12 weeks, as convenient, depending on the context in which they are used.

Each study unit gives an overview of the text at hand before digging into it with a series of questions for reflection or discussion. The unit then concludes by highlighting the gospel of grace in each passage ("Gospel Glimpses"), identifying whole-Bible themes that occur in the passage ("Whole-Bible Connections"), and pinpointing Christian doctrines that are affirmed in the passage ("Theological Soundings").

The final component to each unit is a section for reflecting on personal and practical implications from the passage at hand. The layout provides space for recording responses to the questions proposed, and we think readers need to do this to get the full benefit of the exercise. The series also includes definitions of key words. These definitions are indicated by a note number in the text and are found at the end of each chapter.

Lastly, to help understand the Bible in this deeper way, we urge readers to use the ESV Bible and the *ESV Study Bible*, which are available in various print and digital formats, including online editions at esv.org. The *Knowing the Bible* series is also available online.

May the Lord greatly bless your study as you seek to know him through knowing his Word.

J. I. Packer
Lane T. Dennis

WEEK 1: OVERVIEW

▲

The books of 1 and 2 Samuel were originally compiled as a single book. Modern Hebrew Bibles, in fact, still treat this material as simply "Samuel." These 55 chapters tell the story of an important transitional period of God's plan, centering on the judge/prophet Samuel and the two kings he anointed,[1] Saul and David. In fact, 1–2 Samuel narrates three overlapping but distinct transitions in the leadership of Israel:

- a transition from failing priests to *Samuel*—a righteous judge/prophet and kingmaker;
- a transition from no king to *Saul*—a king of the people's initiative (1 Sam. 8:5);
- and a rather slow transition from Saul to *David*—a king of God's own choosing (1 Sam. 13:14).

Throughout these varied transitions we should certainly observe the negative and positive examples that these leaders provide (see 1 Cor. 10:6, 11). However, a more important matter is *what each transition teaches us about God*. As we shall see in 1–2 Samuel, God is showing not only his power, control, patience, salvation, and righteous judgment but also the fact that he often brings about his purposes in surprising, ironic, and seemingly upside-down ways.

(For further background, see the *ESV Study Bible*, pages 485–490; available online at esv.org.)

Placing 1–2 Samuel in the Larger Story

The books of Samuel concern themselves with God's coming king, a theme with a long history in the Bible. Adam, as God's son and image-bearer, was called to have dominion over creation (Gen. 1:28). He and his offspring were to function as God's vice-regents. When Adam and Eve rebelled, God mercifully promised that through the seed of the woman would come a serpent-crushing offspring (Gen. 3:15). Later, God promised to Abraham not merely the prospect of offspring but also the fact that kings would come from him (Gen. 17:6). His grandson Jacob repeated and specified the kingly promise to his own son Judah: from his line would come a lion-like ruler who would receive the tribute and obedience of the peoples (Gen. 49:8–10). Still later, Moses gave specific directions for the kind of king Israel was to have (Deut. 17:14–20). In short, Israel's king was to be quite different from the kings of the nations around them; he was to be humble and righteous, one "whom the LORD your God will choose" (Deut. 17:15). A king for Israel was always in God's plan; the question was whether Israel would wait on *God's timing* and seek *God's kind of king*.

While 1 Samuel begins at a time in which there is no king in Israel, we soon hear a godly new mother, Hannah, giving thanks to God for far more than simply answering her prayer for a son (1 Sam. 2:1–10). She speaks of the Lord's rescuing the needy and judging the wicked (vv. 3–9), doing so through a future *king*, God's *anointed* (v. 10). Israel's first king, Saul, is not that king. But soon God will prove faithful to his kingly promises through another, David. God later enlarges his royal promises for an *eternal* throne occupied by David's descendants (2 Sam. 7:4–17). Remarkably, David interprets these eternal promises as (literally in Hebrew) a "charter for mankind" (2 Sam. 7:19). Though David is far from perfect, he serves as a true foreshadow of the final and eternal King, Jesus, the Christ, the Son of God and the perfect Son of David (Matt. 1:1; Luke 1:32).

Key Passage

"Not by might shall a man prevail. The adversaries of the LORD shall be broken to pieces; against them he will thunder in heaven. The LORD will judge the ends of the earth; he will give strength to his king and exalt the horn of his anointed." (1 Sam. 2:9b–10; see also 1 Sam. 17:46–47)

Date and Historical Background

The date of composition (or compilation) of 1–2 Samuel is unknown, as is its authorship. The prophet Samuel could not be the author or editor of all of 1–2 Samuel, since his death is recorded in 1 Samuel 25, though he certainly may have been responsible for much of the material occurring prior to 1 Samuel 25.

Authorship and date aside, the timing of the subject matter of 1–2 Samuel clearly records events during the lives of Samuel, Saul, and David (c. 1050–970 BC).

This historical context of 1–2 Samuel illuminates further its place in the history of salvation.[2] While the book of Ruth immediately precedes 1 Samuel in our Bibles, it is Judges that chronologically precedes 1 Samuel. The repeated chorus of Judges is dark, yet it clearly foreshadows what is needed and is soon coming for God's people: "In those days *there was no king in Israel.* Everyone did what was right in his own eyes" (Judges 17:6; 21:25; compare 18:1; 19:1). That said, Ruth also ends with an unmistakable foreshadow of the focal point of the subsequent books, as it concludes with a mention of David (see Ruth 4:17–22).

Outline

I. The Transition to Samuel (1 Samuel 1–7)

    A. Samuel's birth (1 Samuel 1)
    B. Hannah's prayer (1 Sam. 2:1–11)
    C. Eli's worthless sons (1 Sam. 2:12–36)
    D. God speaks through Samuel (1 Samuel 3)
    E. The ark on the move (1 Samuel 4–7)

II. The Transition to Saul (1 Samuel 8–15)

    A. Demand for a king (1 Samuel 8)
    B. Saul's anointing, Samuel's farewell (1 Samuel 9–12)
    C. Saul's sins and rejection as king (2 Samuel 13–15)

III. The Transition to David (1 Samuel 16–2 Samuel 5)

    A. David's anointing (1 Samuel 16)
    B. David and Goliath (1 Samuel 17)
    C. Saul's resentment, Jonathan's commitment (1 Samuel 18–20)
    D. David on the run from Saul (1 Samuel 21–30)
    E. The deaths of Saul and Jonathan (1 Samuel 31–2 Samuel 1)
    F. Conflicts over David's anointing (2 Samuel 2–4)
    G. David fully recognized as king (2 Samuel 5)

IV. David's Kingdom Further Established and Ensured (2 Samuel 6–20)

    A. . . . for God's worship (2 Samuel 6)
    B. . . . by grand promises (2 Samuel 7)
    C. . . . in victory over enemies (2 Samuel 8; 10)
    D. . . . with covenant kindness (2 Samuel 9)
    E. . . . despite great sin (2 Samuel 11–12)
    F. . . . through divine discipline and protection (2 Samuel 12–20)

V. Summary Snapshots of the Davidic Kingdom (2 Samuel 21–24)

    A. Famine and Philistines (2 Samuel 21)
    B. Two final poem-songs (2 Sam. 22:1–23:7)
    C. Mighty men and a costly census (2 Sam. 23:8–24:25)

As You Get Started

Do you have a sense at the outset of this study of the specific emphasis or primary emphases of 1–2 Samuel? Without using your Bible, do any particular passages from 1–2 Samuel come to mind?

Do you know of ways in which the stories of 1–2 Samuel are fulfilled later in the Bible? Based on your current understanding, how might 1–2 Samuel illuminate our understanding of God, Jesus, sin, salvation, or other doctrines?

What aspects of 1–2 Samuel have confused you before? Are there any specific questions you hope to have answered through this study?

As You Finish This Unit . . .

Take a few minutes to ask God to bless you with increased understanding and a transformed heart and life as you begin this study of 1–2 Samuel.

Definitions

[1] **Anoint** – In Scripture, to pour oil (usually olive oil) on someone or something to set the person or thing apart for a special purpose. Anointing was performed for the high priest, for tabernacle vessels, for kings, and for prophets. The Hebrew word *Messiah* and its Greek equivalent *Christ* both mean "anointed one."

[2] **History of salvation** – God's unified plan for all of history to accomplish the salvation of his people. He accomplished this salvation in the work of Jesus Christ on earth by his life, crucifixion, burial, and resurrection (Eph. 1:3–23). The consummation of God's plan will take place when Jesus Christ comes again to establish the "new heavens and a new earth in which righteousness dwells" (2 Pet. 3:13).

Week 2: New Beginnings: Hannah, Eli, and Samuel

1 Samuel 1–3

▲

The Place of the Passage

The first three chapters of 1 Samuel introduce us to a coming transition in Israel's leadership. Eli was a judge and priest. His sons (also priests) were "worthless men" (2:12), and Eli "did not restrain" their scandalous behavior (3:13). God was about to judge the house of Eli and replace their leadership with a godly young man, Samuel, who would be a true prophet. Samuel would hear from God and speak God's words to all Israel (3:21–4:1). Chapter 1 begins by telling us of Samuel's miraculous birth, born to a godly, suffering, prayerful woman, Hannah. Her prayer of response (2:1–10) is more than her own personal thanks for a son, as it foreshadows the primary themes of 1–2 Samuel.

The Big Picture

Closing the door on the dark days of the judges, God is beginning something new—vindicating the afflicted, judging ungodly leaders, and speaking afresh to his people through a new young prophet, Samuel.

Reflection and Discussion

Read through the complete passage for this study, 1 Samuel 1–3. Then review the questions below concerning this section of 1–2 Samuel and write your notes on them. (For further background, see the *ESV Study Bible*, pages 491-497; available online at esv.org.)

1. Hannah's Prayer and Praise (1:1–2:10)

Hannah's struggle with barrenness (not to mention other difficulties in her home life) is, sadly, something that many women can relate to, even today. Her life of godliness and persistent prayer is certainly a model for anyone suffering similarly. However, much more than one woman's suffering and prayers is going on in these early chapters. Some of the greatest clues are in her prayer-song (2:1–10). List some of the elements of her prayer that seem surprisingly grand and far-reaching, considering the occasion.

Some have suggested that Hannah's prayer (2:1–10) functions almost as a thematic table of contents for 1–2 Samuel. What themes do you see emphasized in Hannah's prayer?

Another prayer-song is found in these books: 2 Samuel 22:1–51, written by King David. What do Hannah's and David's prayers have in common? Compare especially the beginning and ending of the two prayers.

Comparing 1 Samuel 2:9–10 and 2 Samuel 22:47–51 specifically, do you detect any differences between the two prayers? In other words, what has changed from the beginning to the end of these books?

It is significant to find similar poetic prayer-songs at the beginning and end of a narrative book (remember to think of 1–2 Samuel as essentially one book). What might these "bookends" imply for the rest of 1–2 Samuel?

----

2. Contrasting Samuel with Eli's Sons (2:11–36)

The rest of chapter 2 repeatedly contrasts Samuel with Eli's sons. What are these contrasts, and what do they signify?

----

3. Samuel's Calling as Prophet (3:1–4:1a)

Compare and contrast the beginning (3:1) and end (3:20–4:1a) of Samuel's calling. In a few words, describe what this section is really about. What change takes place between 3:1 and 3:20–4:1a, and what significance might this change have?

Look back at Hannah's prayer (2:1–10). What connections do you see between her words and what takes place in the rest of our passage (2:11–4:1a)?

Read through the following three sections on *Gospel Glimpses, Whole-Bible Connections*, and *Theological Soundings*. Then take time to consider the *Personal Implications* these sections may have for you.

▶ Gospel Glimpses

NOT BY MIGHT. This little line from Hannah's prayer—"not by might" (1 Sam. 2:9)—is important for the narratives in 1–2 Samuel; it is a truth demonstrated again and again. God's way of working is not according to the world's wisdom. His power does not need to *look* powerful—in fact, he most often chooses to show his power through apparent weakness. This is a motif stretching through the whole Bible, with Jesus and the salvation he brings as consummate examples. Not only was the Messiah born into obscurity, poverty, and rejection (see, e.g., Matthew 1; Luke 2); the message of "Christ crucified" is "a stumbling block to Jews and folly to Gentiles, but to those who are called" it is "the power of God" for salvation (1 Cor. 1:23–24). The cross proves that God saves in such a way that we can only "boast in the Lord" (1 Cor. 1:31). In fact, this is how God continues to save us and work through us—his "power is made perfect in weakness" (2 Cor. 12:9).

REVERSALS. One way of describing these early chapters of 1 Samuel is with the word *reversal*. Hannah receives a reversal of fortune—from marginalized and mocked to blessed and honored (ch. 1). Her prayer of response contains a string of various reversals the Lord brings about (2:4–8). These chapters also witness the beginning of a transition in the leadership of Israel, from the wayward house of Eli to godly young Samuel (which will decisively unfold in chapters 3–7). But even now, through Samuel another great reversal takes place when God begins to speak afresh (ch. 3), marking the end of a *word-less* era and the dawn of a *word-full* era. Yet, as important as these events were in their day, they foreshadow a greater series of reversals that takes place when the true and final King ends 400 years of prophetic silence as the incarnate Word (John 1:14), judging another era of ungodly spiritual leaders and ushering in a new priesthood with himself at the center.

▶ Whole-Bible Connections

FROM BARRENNESS TO BIRTH. Hannah's story of barrenness-to-birth is one of several in the Bible. All are significant and occur at key moments, with key people. Abraham's wife, Sarah, was barren until, late in life, God opened her womb and gave them Isaac (Genesis 18–21). Isaac's wife, Rebekah, was barren until the Lord blessed her with Jacob and Esau (Genesis 25). Jacob's wife Rachel struggled with infertility, but eventually the Lord provided Joseph and Benjamin (Genesis 30; 35). Samson's mother was barren until an angel announced a coming son (Judges 13). In the New Testament, Elizabeth was past childbearing years when an angel announced the miraculous conception of one who would prepare the way for the Messiah (Luke 1). And, of course, her cousin Mary, though not barren, encountered an angel who announced the even more significant conception of the Christ-child in her virgin womb. What is the significance of these similar events? God's promises have always centered on a seed, a son ("offspring"; Gen. 3:15). God was faithful to keep his plan moving along, even when hope seemed barren, impossible. In time, God intervened; he provided. Then, "[W]hen the fullness of time had come, God sent forth his Son, born of a woman" (Gal. 4:4).

A REVERBERATING SONG. Hannah's important prayer-song seems to lean upon Moses' Song (Exodus 15). Similarly, Mary leans upon Hannah's prayer for her famous song in response to Gabriel's announcement (Luke 1:45–56). Not surprisingly, his announcement to Mary includes references to David and the Davidic covenant[1] (2 Sam. 7:4–17): "He will be great and will be called the Son of the Most High. And the Lord God will give to him *the throne of his father David*, and he will reign over the house of Jacob forever, and *of his kingdom there will be no end*" (Luke 1:32–33). As noted earlier, Hannah's prayer reverberates throughout the pages of 1–2 Samuel. But it has even farther-reaching implications—looking back to Moses and the exodus and reaching ahead through Mary to the virgin birth of the eternal Son of David.

Theological Soundings

ANSWER TO PRAYER. We know from experience that God's responses to prayer can be rather mysterious. God knows infinitely more than we do. He does not have only our happiness or personal fulfillment in mind but also our eternal good, linked to a grand plan involving countless interrelated people, events, purposes, and problems. James teaches that, sometimes, "You do not have, because you do not ask," while other times, "You ask and do not receive, because you ask wrongly, to spend it on your passions" (James 4:2–3). God sometimes says no to our petitions for our own good, however mysterious that may be to us. On the other hand, God does seem to be attuned particularly to fervent prayers of the righteous (James 5:16–18). He can be honored by persistence in prayer, especially when one prays for something such as justice, as in the parable of the persistent widow (Luke 18:1–8). These and other passages shed some light on God's answer to Hannah's godly, persistent prayers (1 Samuel 1). But they do not provide a foolproof recipe for always getting what we ask for. Remember that when Jesus—even Jesus!—petitioned his Father in the garden, he added, "Nevertheless, not my will, but yours, be done" (Luke 22:42). Let us marvel, and also follow his lead.

Personal Implications

Take time to reflect on the implications of 1 Samuel 1–3 for your own life today. Consider what you have learned that might lead you to praise God, repent of sin, and trust more deeply in his gracious promises. Write down your reflections under the three headings we have considered and on the passage as a whole.

1. Gospel Glimpses

2. Whole-Bible Connections

3. Theological Soundings

4. 1 Samuel 1–3

> ### As You Finish This Unit . . .

Take a moment now to ask for the Lord's blessing and help as you continue in this study of 1–2 Samuel. And take a moment also to look back through this unit of study, to reflect on some key things that the Lord may be teaching you.

Definition

[1] **Covenant** – A binding agreement between two parties, typically involving a formal statement of their relationship, a list of stipulations and obligations for both parties, a list of witnesses to the agreement, and a list of curses for unfaithfulness and blessings for faithfulness to the agreement.

Week 3: Israel Defeated, God Defeating

1 Samuel 4–7

▲

Although the *word* of the Lord has returned to Israel (1 Sam. 3:19–20), the *glory* of Israel is about to depart (4:21). Trusting in the ark of the covenant as a good-luck charm, Israel is trounced by the Philistines, who also steal the ark. Eli and his sons die, fulfilling the judgment foretold (3:13–14). God is *breaking to pieces* his enemies (2:10)—enemies abroad and at home. But the capture of the ark is far from a defeat of God, who can defeat thousands of Philistines without the help of a single Israelite (ch. 5). The Philistines, and later the Israelites, learn that the presence of God is no trifling matter (ch. 6). While Israel can find no immediate solution for the problems caused by the ark's dwelling among them (6:19–21), Samuel leads the nation in repentance, restoration, and renewal of their covenant with God (7:3–17).

The Big Picture

God will not allow himself to be anyone's good-luck charm (1 Sam. 4:3), trophy (5:2), or novelty (6:19), but he will hear and help a repentant people who call out to him (7:8–13).

> ### Reflection and Discussion

Read through the complete passage for this study, 1 Samuel 4–7. Then review the questions below concerning this section of 1–2 Samuel and write your notes on them. (For further background, see the *ESV Study Bible*, pages 497–503; available online at esv.org.)

1. The Ark Captured (ch. 4)

Samuel's prophetic ministry is celebrated by the nation in 3:19–21. But, although there are several dilemmas for the people over the next couple of chapters (4:2–7:2), there is no mention of the prophet Samuel. What might be the significance of this fact for the opening scene of our passage (4:1–3)?

It was suggested above that when the elders call for the ark to go before them in battle, they are trusting in the ark as something like a good-luck charm. This was not always the case; sometimes the ark rightly led the way into battle (e.g., Joshua 6). But read 1 Samuel 4:3 carefully. What in this verse suggests that the elders trust the ark of God more than the God of the ark?

Giving the name "Ichabod" to a newborn child (4:19–22) indicates how devastating the capture of the ark is for Israel. Based on your present knowledge of the ark, why is its capture and removal so significant?

2. The Ark among the Philistines (ch. 5)

While Israel's defeat and the ark's capture seem like setbacks, even embarrassments, it is soon clear that God is orchestrating it all. There are at least four statements in chapter 5 that make God's sovereign purposes explicit. Where are those statements?

In 1–2 Samuel God often reveals himself in ironic or surprising ways. List some of the ironic elements of the incident with Dagon in 5:1–5.

Dagon's loss of hands (5:4) is one such irony, particularly in light of the rest of the chapter. How are Dagon's severed hands contrasted with another's "hand" in 5:6–11?

God can accomplish many goals at the same time, even with the same events. List four or five of the things God is accomplishing in chapters 4 and 5. Are these things apparent to the participants in the narrative?

3. The Ark Returned to Israel (ch. 6)

The men of Beth-shemesh rejoiced to see the ark returning (6:13), but their joy turned quickly to mourning when some "looked upon" the ark and were struck dead (6:19). Why was a mere *look* so deadly? (See Num. 4:19–20; 1 Sam. 6:20a; 2 Sam. 6:7.)

In chapter 4, the elders sent for the ark so that "it" might save them (v. 3). But when the ark returns to Israel in chapter 6 and soon proves deadly, they soon wonder, "to whom shall *he* go up away from us?" (v. 20). What is so tragic about the different words ("it" in 4:3 and "he" in 6:20) in each context?

4. Israel's Repentance and Restoration (ch. 7)

Based on 1 Samuel 7:1–3, how would you describe the spiritual state of Israel at this time?

Based on the rest of chapter 7, how would you describe (a) the nation's response to Samuel's call to repentance and (b) the results that follow?

Remembering that Hannah's prayer foreshadowed many events to follow, reread 2:1–10 and write down connections you find there with chapters 4–7.

Read through the following three sections on *Gospel Glimpses*, *Whole-Bible Connections*, and *Theological Soundings*. Then take time to consider the *Personal Implications* these sections may have for you.

Gospel Glimpses

THE PROBLEM OF GOD'S PRESENCE. Adam and Eve were created to experience and enjoy the presence of God, but when they sinned, they rightly felt guilt, shame, and estrangement from him. They covered themselves; they fled and hid. Of course, God came to them and spoke words of judgment *and* hope (Gen. 3:16–19). But since all of their offspring (save one) have been born as sinners, their offspring are in a similar position of estrangement from God—even *enmity* (i.e., hostility or hatred) with him (see Gen. 3:15). There is a path to hope, indeed, but it starts with recognition that God's presence is actually a problem for sinners. God is completely pure; evil "may not dwell" with him (Ps. 5:4). This is what the Philistines learn when they take the ark home. Wherever it goes, judgment is severe, even deadly (1 Sam. 5:11–12). The question asked by the men of Beth-shemesh summarizes the problem for every sinner: "Who is able to stand before the LORD, this holy God?" (1 Sam. 6:20). The answer, of course, is that none of us can. Tragically, when left to ourselves, we flee from God and stay in hiding from him; or worse—if we could, we would actually send God away!

THE PATHWAY TO GOD'S PRESENCE. The problem of God's presence among sinners is not something that can be covered over with fig leaves (Gen. 3:7) or passed off to someone else (1 Sam. 5:8, 10). But when we bring our sin before the Lord openly, confess it, and desire to turn from it (1 Sam. 7:3–6), our sin and guilt can be covered. As David testified, "When I kept silent, my bones wasted away through my groaning all day long." But "I acknowledged my sin to you, and I did not cover my iniquity; I said, 'I will confess my transgressions to the LORD,' and you forgave the iniquity of my sin" (Ps. 32:3, 5). Indeed how happy "is the one . . . whose sin is covered" (Ps. 32:1). For those who have so confessed their sin and turned to God for forgiveness, his presence can then actually be a sweet "hiding place" as he *surrounds* his people with "shouts of deliverance" (Ps. 32:7).

▶ Whole-Bible Connections

THE ARK, THE PRESENCE, AND THE BLOOD. The ark was the symbol of God's mediated presence, by which God makes his presence known among his people. Angels adorned the sides, signifying that the top was like God's throne or footstool. It was also on top of the ark that sacrificial blood was poured out on the Day of Atonement,[1] signifying the covering of the people's sin and guilt. God has never forgiven sin by sweeping it under some cosmic rug. We read in Hebrews, "Without the shedding of blood there is no forgiveness of sins" (Heb. 9:22). This principle was demonstrated in the coverings God made for Adam and Eve after the fall[2] (Gen. 3:21), in the blood applied to doorposts on the night of the Passover (Exodus 12), and in the many blood sacrifices made by priests throughout the time of the old covenant. Yet, although these rituals taught Israel much about sin and sacrifice, they could not completely take away sin; they were merely foreshadows of the perfect, final sacrifice of Jesus. Only his blood can cover sin once and for all, and provide access to God's presence (see Heb. 9:24–28; 10:18–22).

THE STUPIDITY OF IDOLATRY. The Philistines think they have beaten Israel's God. They take the ark and put it in the temple of their god Dagon, as if the ark were *his* trophy. But God will not be mocked—in fact, he makes a mockery of such idol-foolery. The next morning, the statue of Dagon is facedown before the ark, as if bowing before the true God (5:3). The Philistines have to "put [Dagon] back in his place," proving that their "god" is utterly helpless. This is even clearer the next morning when Dagon is again found facedown, but this time without hands or head. Read Psalm 115, which contrasts worthless idols with the true God. Then remember that Christians still today must "flee from idolatry" (1 Cor. 10:14; compare 1 John 5:21). We flee idols in part by remembering that idols in every form and every age are a senseless thing to trust in.

▶ Theological Soundings

GOD'S MYSTERIOUS, MULTIFACETED WAYS. Romans 11 ends with words that could well summarize the roller-coaster ride of 1 Samuel 4–7: "Oh, the depth of the riches and wisdom and knowledge of God! How unsearchable are his judgments and how inscrutable his ways!" (Rom. 11:33–34). God had promised victory over the enemy and for his presence to remain with his people (e.g., Deut. 31:5–8). Yet, in 1 Samuel 4:10, thirty thousand Israelites are slain, and the ark is taken away by pagan enemies. This seems unthinkable. But God is up to more than anyone could imagine. He is teaching his people painfully not to presume upon their God, nor to trust the ark as if it were a lucky rabbit's foot. He is also fulfilling the promise of judgment on Eli and his wicked sons, replacing their weak, wicked leadership with a true prophet of God, Samuel. The ark's capture and relocation to Philistine land provides a profound example of the Lord's fierce power and confounding ways. Like a terrifying game of hot-potato, the ark is passed from one city to the next until the Philistines rightly send it back to Israel. God is always doing many things at once. We do not get to see it all, but 1 Samuel 4–7 provides a window into his mysterious, multifaceted ways.

Personal Implications

Take time to reflect on the implications of 1 Samuel 4–7 for your own life today. Consider what you have learned that might lead you to praise God, repent of sin, and trust more deeply in his gracious promises. Write down your reflections under the three headings we have considered and on the passage as a whole.

1. Gospel Glimpses

2. Whole-Bible Connections

3. Theological Soundings

4. 1 Samuel 4–7

_____

_____

_____

_____

_____

_____

▶ **As You Finish This Unit . . .**

Take a moment now to ask for the Lord's blessing and help as you continue in this study of 1–2 Samuel. And take a moment also to look back through this unit of study, to reflect on some key things that the Lord may be teaching you.

Definitions

[1] **Day of Atonement** – The holiest day in the Israelite calendar, the day on which atonement was made for all the sins of Israel from the past year (Leviticus 16). It occurred on the tenth day of the seventh month, and all Israel was to fast and do no work. Only on that day each year could someone—the high priest—enter the Most Holy Place of the tabernacle (later, the temple) and offer the necessary sacrifices.

[2] **The fall** – Adam and Eve's disobedience of God by eating the fruit from the tree of the knowledge of good and evil, resulting in their loss of innocence and favor with God and the introduction of sin and its effects into the world.

WEEK 4: SAUL'S RISE, THEN REJECTION

1 Samuel 8–15

▲

First Samuel 7 ended with the summary, "Samuel judged Israel all the days of his life" (v. 15). But the elders of Israel are worried about what might happen to the leadership of Israel after Samuel departs from the scene. And so, in chapter 8, they demand a king "like all the nations" (v. 5). In a response of judgment to this request, God gives them exactly what they desire: a king like those of the other nations. Although this king—Saul—looks somewhat promising at first (chs. 9–11), it is soon clear that he is neither faithful nor full of faith (chs. 13–15). Thus God will "tear" the kingdom from Saul and give it to another, "a man after his own heart" (13:14; 15:28). This begins Saul's downward spiral into self and sin, charted in the rest of 1 Samuel.

The Big Picture

Israel's first king, Saul, is not the long-awaited promised king (see Gen. 49:10) but rather one who reflects Israel's weak faith in the Lord.

> ## Reflection and Discussion

Read through the complete passage for this study, 1 Samuel 8–15. Then review the questions below concerning this section of 1–2 Samuel and write your notes on them. (For further background, see the *ESV Study Bible*, pages 503–517; available online at esv.org.)

1. The Demand for a King (ch. 8)

Are the concerns stated by the elders about the future leadership of Israel legitimate (8:1–3)? How might the elders have dealt better with their concerns? (Language from ch. 7 will be useful here.)

Read Deuteronomy 17:14–20 with 1 Samuel 8 in mind. What is wrong about Israel's demand for a king? What contrasts do you see between these two passages?

What do you think is meant by these statements: "a king . . . like all the nations" (v. 5), "that we also may be like all the nations," and "that our king may . . . go out before us and fight our battles" (v. 20)? Why is this tantamount to rejecting God (v. 7)?

Samuel's warning about the kind of king they demand (vv. 10–18) repeats a key word six times. What is this word, and what is its significance here?

How should we understand God's granting Israel's desire for a king? (Read Rom. 1:24, 26, 28 before you answer.)

-----

2. Saul's Anointing and Early Success (chs. 9–12)

Chapters 9–10 comprise a long, winding road leading to Saul's anointing and public announcement as king. The details are at times confusing, but the primary point is God's sovereign orchestration. Reread 9:15–10:16 and note explicit mentions of God's sovereign control.

Our first introduction to Saul emphasizes his appearance: he is the handsomest, tallest Israelite (9:2). Even Samuel finds Saul's appearance impressive (10:23–24). But why is this emphasized? How might chapter 8 and Hannah's prayer (2:1–11) shed light on the emphasis on Saul's stature?

It is curious that Saul will not tell his uncle about his anointing (10:16), and it is curious that he is hiding among the baggage before his public announcement as king (10:22). What might these small details suggest about Saul?

Chapter 11 is surprisingly optimistic. But should we consider Samuel's warnings of 8:10–18 to now be moot? Based on 9:16 and chapter 11, how do you see God showing mercy to his people even amid his discipline of them?

3. Saul's Faithless Failures and Rejection (chs. 13–15)

Chapter 13 begins with a successful battle against the Philistines. Who is responsible, humanly speaking, for leading the victory? Who takes credit for the victory?

A contrast between Saul and his son Jonathan continues throughout chapters 13–14. What contrasts do you notice?

What is wrong with Saul's offering a sacrifice in 13:8–9? What motivates his decision to make a sacrifice before Samuel's arrival?

While chapter 14 continues to expose Saul's foolishness and tyrant-like behavior, chapter 15 is the breaking point. According to 15:1–19, what is Saul's failure that leads to the final judgment against his kingship?

What should we make of Saul's response to Samuel's confrontation (15:20–21)? Do you take Saul's confessions in 15:24–30 to be genuine repentance? Are there any indications concerning its genuineness in the context?

Read through the following three sections on *Gospel Glimpses*, *Whole-Bible Connections*, and *Theological Soundings*. Then take time to consider the *Personal Implications* these sections may have for you.

Gospel Glimpses

GODLY VERSUS WORLDLY SORROW. We must distinguish worldly sorrow, which leads to death, from godly sorrow, which leads to true repentance[1] (2 Cor. 7:10). In 1 Samuel 13, Saul is confronted by the prophet but is obviously not repentant. In chapter 15, when confronted he responds with some sorrowful language, but also makes excuses, blames others (vv. 21, 24), and seems concerned to save face above anything else (v. 30). With these clues, along with Samuel's reactions to them, it seems clear that Saul is displaying worldly sorrow, not true repentance. The difference is of utter importance. Repentance is required of all who would bring their sin to Jesus for forgiveness (Mark 1:15). It is required, but this requirement is also a gracious invitation. How marvelous that we can bring our sin to God! How frightening, conversely, to hold onto and hide our sin, as if we could!

A KING UNLIKE THE NATIONS' KINGS. As it goes with God's king, so it will go with his people. This principle can be observed throughout redemptive history, particularly in 1 Samuel 8–15. When Saul is obedient, courageous, and merciful, all goes well for Israel (ch. 11). But when he is selfish, fearful, proud, and disobedient, he brings upheaval upon the whole kingdom (ch. 15). This is what the kings of the nations are like: self-willed, self-serving, and self-reliant, even though they may look impressive (8:10–18). Jesus is a king *most unlike* the kings of this world. He is indeed a king (*the* King), even though he did not look like a king in the world's eyes. He came "not to be served but to serve, and to give his life as a ransom for many" (Mark 10:45). The kings of this world take and take and take, but King Jesus gives and gives and gives. Sinners who place themselves under this humble, righteous King not only receive grace but also are transformed by his otherworldly outlook of glory through service (Mark 10:42–44; Phil. 2:3–11).

Whole-Bible Connections

THE ONE TO COME. "Are you the one who is to come, or shall we look for another?" (Matt. 11:3). This question put to Jesus by John the Baptist's disciples could have been asked of many figures throughout the Old Testament as well. As discussed in Week 1, God's people had long awaited a seed, a son, a ruler (Gen. 3:15; 15:4; 49:10). As Balaam prophesied, a star would rise out of the line of Jacob to crush the enemy and establish dominion (Num. 24:17–19). First Samuel opens with Hannah's speaking of a future king (2:10). Despite Israel's sinful demand for a king (ch. 8), Saul is, for a time, a king used of God to unite God's people and defeat their enemies (ch. 11). But in the next few chapters it becomes increasingly clear that Saul is not the long-awaited promised king, not even a decent king. First Samuel 16 will introduce us to another, soon-to-be king who in many ways will (for a time) fulfill properly the old promise of a righteous ruler. And yet, King David is neither perfect nor eternal. Only Jesus, the eternal, perfect son of David was and is "the One." Praise God we no longer have to wonder or wait.

AN ETERNAL RULER. The prophet Samuel was used mightily of the Lord (3:19; 7:15). He delivered God's word judicially and led the nation spiritually. And he did so "all the days of his life" (7:15). Note those words carefully. They highlight God's kindness through Samuel's fidelity and longevity while also subtly reminding us that Samuel, too, was a sinner whose days would came to an end. More tragically, his sons (and successors) were wicked (8:3). Succession of leadership can be a real problem. While God may raise up a godly leader for a time, his sons might be wicked. That is why Jesus' perfect, eternal, unchanging, unthreatened kingdom is so utterly unique and important. Indeed, this is heaven's chorus: "And he shall reign forever and ever" (Rev. 11:15).

> ## Theological Soundings

THE LORD REGRETTED. Twice God states that he regretted Saul's kingship (15:11, 35). These statements come in the same chapter in which Samuel claims that God is "not a man that he should have regret" (v. 29). The same Hebrew word is found in all three instances, but it can be rightly translated as either "regretted" or "grieved" (e.g., Gen. 6:6). While God is never surprised by turns of events, nor wishes to go back in time to do things differently, he is genuinely *grieved* by human sin and its effects. On the other hand, because God knows and plans all things (Isa. 46:9–10), he is not like human beings, who frequently regret, change their minds, and wish to go back and do things differently. Mysteriously, our God truly grieves sin but does not regret any of his all-wise decisions.

DESTRUCTION OF AMALEKITES. Saul's greatest sin in these chapters is holding back from destroying *all* of the Amalekites. God commanded, "Do not spare them" (15:3). But how can a righteous and compassionate God decree such actions? This is a difficult question, but a number of related matters must be kept in mind. (1) God is the righteous and just creator of all, even when we question it. (2) Everyone is born in rebellion against God, deserving his full and immediate judgment; no one *deserves* mercy. (3) The Amalekites were an especially wicked people whom God had promised long ago to "blot out" (Deut. 25:19); thus, he was remarkably patient with their judgment. (4) God intended to use Israel as an imperfect instrument of judgment on the Amalekites in order to restrain evil in the world and provide his people with a sacred land for his presence and blessing. (5) Foreshadowings of the final, end-time judgment (and blessing) are found throughout history. In the end, all of humanity will be separated into heaven and hell. (6) Jesus came to deal with the deeper problems of sin, Satan, and death. Because he has conquered these foes through his death and resurrection, his followers are not called to fight with swords (John 18:36), let alone wipe out whole nations, but to take good news (and warnings) to all peoples (Col. 1:28).

> ## Personal Implications

Take time to reflect on the implications of 1 Samuel 8–15 for your own life today. Consider what you have learned that might lead you to praise God, repent of sin, and trust more deeply in his gracious promises. Write down your reflections under the three headings we have considered and on the passage as a whole.

1. Gospel Glimpses

2. Whole-Bible Connections

3. Theological Soundings

4. 1 Samuel 8–15

> ### As You Finish This Unit . . .

Take a moment now to ask for the Lord's blessing and help as you continue in this study of 1–2 Samuel. And take a moment also to look back through this unit of study, to reflect on some key things that the Lord may be teaching you.

Definition

[1] **Repentance** – A complete change of heart and mind regarding one's overall attitude toward God or one's individual actions. True regeneration and conversion is always accompanied by repentance.

WEEK 5: DAVID'S RISE, SAUL'S RESENTMENT

1 Samuel 16–20

▲

Twice the prophet Samuel has told Saul that God has rejected him because of his sin; his kingdom will be "torn" from him and given to "a man after [God's] own heart" (13:13–14; 15:28). Now we are introduced to this coming, better king (ch. 16). Unlike the outwardly impressive Saul, David is the last-born and likely the smallest of his brothers. But "the LORD is with him" (16:18), as is evident in his courageous stand for the Lord against the giant Philistine (ch. 17). As David's success, fame, and alliances grow, so do Saul's envy, fear, and schemes against David (ch. 18). His murderous intentions force David to flee, a drama played out in the rest of 1 Samuel.

The Big Picture

The Lord's anointed (see 2:10) finally comes on the scene, with glad recognition by some (especially Jonathan) but with great opposition from others (especially Saul).

> ## Reflection and Discussion

Read through the complete passage for this study, 1 Samuel 16–20. Then review the questions below concerning this section of 1–2 Samuel and write your notes on them. (For further background, see the *ESV Study Bible*, pages 517–526; available online at esv.org.)

1. David's Anointing (ch. 16)

According to 16:6–7, why did Samuel assume that Jesse's son Eliab would be the one he should anoint as king? Where have we seen a similar dynamic earlier in 1 Samuel?

What does it say about Jesse's estimation of David that he is not brought in from the fields for this momentous occasion (16:10–11)? Note that Jesse seems a bit dismissive of Samuel's inquiry as to whether he has another son.

What in Hannah's prayer (2:1–10) helps to illuminate this scene of anointing in Bethlehem?

God's Spirit "rushed upon" Saul in earlier chapters (10:10; 11:6), but something more is said about the Spirit's presence in regard to David (16:13). What is it? What does it signify that the Spirit came upon David (v. 13) and departed from Saul (v. 14)?

2. David's Victory over Goliath (ch. 17)

While David's famous battle with the Philistine giant is what we might remember most from this chapter, it is described only briefly (vv. 48–51). Three speeches given by David (vv. 26, 32–37, 45–47) provide the interpretive key to these events. What do the speeches have in common? What is at the heart of David's willingness to fight the giant?

Throughout this chapter, David's confidence in the Lord is contrasted with others' paralyzing fear. According to verses 11 and 24, who is afraid? According to verse 16, for how many days had Goliath challenged and taunted the Israelites?

King Saul should have been the one to fight Goliath (see 8:20; 9:16; 10:23). What does it say about Saul that he is so quickly willing to let a young, small shepherd go out to fight a giant (vv. 33–37)? How does this relate to Saul's putting his armor on David (vv. 38–39)?

In David's final speech (vv. 46–47) he explains that there will be two audiences for the spectacle of Goliath's coming defeat, and a specific message for each audience. Who are the audiences, and what is the message for each?

In light of your study of this chapter, how has your understanding of the David and Goliath story changed or been enriched?

3. David and the Division of Saul's House (ch. 18–20)

While Saul technically remains king, he looks increasingly less like Israel's ideal king, while David increasingly demonstrates the traits of a godly king. Provide examples of each from chapter 18.

As heir apparent to his father's throne, Jonathan provides significant gifts to David in 18:4. What do they signify? (See 20:13–17, 30 for help.)

Saul's emotional state is referenced a number of times (see 18:8, 10, 12, 15, 29). Do you see any pattern or trajectory in these verses?

Multiple times we are told that Saul "had his spear in his hand" (18:10; 19:9; also 22:6), but in each case, Saul is not on a battlefield. What might this signify about Saul?

Read Psalm 59, which is David's poetic reflection upon the dangers recounted in 1 Samuel 19. What in the psalm strikes you as particularly relevant or illuminating for understanding the events of 1 Samuel 19?

Read through the following three sections on *Gospel Glimpses, Whole-Bible Connections,* and *Theological Soundings*. Then take time to consider the *Personal Implications* these sections may have for you.

Gospel Glimpses

WE NEED HELP. Chapter 17 of 1 Samuel is not so much about David's great faith, let alone about how one overcomes social and physical obstacles. It is rather about David's great God overcoming his enemies for his name's sake.

But God does so, in this case, through a future king who will lead and rescue his people. First Samuel began with a visionary prayer for God to judge the proud, break the bows of the mighty, and bring down and raise up (2:3–6). It is not by might that a man prevails; the Lord will thunder against his enemies as he gives strength to his king and exalts his anointed (2:9–10). These hopes are beginning to be realized in God's work through his servant David. David's zealous faith is impressive, but before we can ever begin to imitate it (even in small ways) we must first come to recognize our more appropriate place in the story. We are often like the soldiers, David's brothers, and Saul—cowering in fear, frozen in our unbelief. We, too, need a Savior to come, to conquer, to rescue. David's greater son, Jesus, has done just that—stepping in on our behalf to conquer the giant threats of Satan, sin, and death (see Heb. 2:14–15). "Thanks be to God, who gives us the victory through our Lord" (1 Cor. 15:57).

GIVING UP A KINGDOM. Jonathan willingly abdicates his future right to the throne because he recognizes David as God's true anointed. Giving David his robe, armor, and sword (emblems of his position as crown prince) is an act of great faith, with great risk. He is identifying himself with David over his own father. This is the only proper thing to do, but it is remarkable. This situation is almost like a parable[1] for how Jesus calls would-be followers into his kingdom: "Whoever loves father or mother more than me is not worthy of me" (Matt. 10:37). Homes will be divided on account of Christ. However, "Everyone who has left houses . . . or father . . . , for my name's sake, will receive a hundredfold and will inherit eternal life" (Matt. 19:29). Learn from Jonathan and Jesus: abandon your shaky little kingdom for his, no matter the risk or cost.

> ## Whole-Bible Connections

PSALM 2. Like Hannah's prayer, Psalm 2 is another passage that reverberates throughout Scripture. It was written for the installment of Davidic kings based on the promises God gives to David in 2 Samuel 7:4–17 concerning his throne and offspring. Although the composition of Psalm 2 came after the events of our chapters in Samuel, its truths are ever-present. "The kings of the earth [like Saul] set themselves . . . against the LORD and against his Anointed" (Ps. 2:2). But "He who sits in the heavens laughs"; God *will* "set [his] King on Zion" (Ps. 2:4, 6). So all would-be rulers must either "kiss the Son" (a symbol of allegiance and honor) and find blessed refuge in him, or "perish" (Ps. 2:12). Jonathan chooses the former, while his father seems to be heading headlong toward the latter. Of course, Psalm 2 reverberates throughout Scripture in the other direction, too. Its crescendo is found in the great Son of David and Son of God, Jesus. Psalm 2 explains the wicked rejection and crucifixion of Jesus (see Acts 4:24–28). But that cross was also the very means by which God would install his king and provide refuge for all who recognize Jesus as the true King. Those who will not recognize him aright, however, will perish. Psalm 2 reverberates not only throughout Scripture but also into eternity.

Theological Soundings

A HARMFUL SPIRIT. It may be alarming to read that a "harmful spirit from the LORD tormented" Saul (16:14). This raises a number of questions concerning God's sovereignty,[2] some of which cannot be answered fully. But a number of biblical truths can help to clarify what this does and does not mean. God himself does no evil, and he does not tempt (James 1:13). But, mysteriously, he does use various forces of evil to accomplish his purposes without himself tempting or doing evil. The cross was the ultimate example of this (Acts 2:23; 4:27–28). Judas's betrayal of Jesus is in a similar vein (John 13:18–19). Sinners and demons are responsible for their sin, but the Lord plans their sin for his wise, righteous purposes—in this case, as part of his judgment of Saul for his belligerent activity detailed in 1 Samuel 13–15.

Personal Implications

Take time to reflect on the implications of 1 Samuel 16–20 for your own life today. Consider what you have learned that might lead you to praise God, repent of sin, and trust more deeply in his gracious promises. Write down your reflections under the three headings we have considered and on the passage as a whole.

1. Gospel Glimpses

2. Whole-Bible Connections

3. Theological Soundings

4. 1 Samuel 16–20

> ## As You Finish This Unit . . .

Take a moment now to ask for the Lord's blessing and help as you continue in this study of 1–2 Samuel. And take a moment also to look back through this unit of study, to reflect on some key things that the Lord may be teaching you.

Definitions

[1] **Parable** – A story that uses everyday imagery and activities to communicate a spiritual truth. Jesus often taught in parables (e.g., Matthew 13).

[2] **Sovereignty** – Supreme and independent power and authority. Sovereignty over all things is a distinctive attribute of God (1 Tim. 6:15–16). He directs all things in order to carry out his purposes (Rom. 8:28–29).

WEEK 6: SAUL'S PURSUIT, DAVID'S PROTECTION

1 Samuel 21–26

▲

The Place of the Passage

With Saul's murderous intentions now undeniable (1 Sam. 19:1; 20:33), David is on the run for his life. Saul's manhunt is menacing but ultimately futile, for God faithfully protects and provides for his anointed. In fact, by extension, David will soon protect and provide for God's people (ch. 22). In great contrast, Saul ravages them. This contrast between two "kings" will grow more stark throughout the rest of 1 Samuel: Saul's self-focus, fear, and jealousy take him deeper into sin and spiritual darkness, while David's trust in God shines brightly amid the darkest of these circumstances.

The Big Picture

God's chosen and anointed one, David, is opposed and in constant danger, but God is with him—a truth increasingly recognized in Israel but more severely opposed by a desperate Saul.

41

> **Reflection and Discussion**

Read through the complete passage for this study, 1 Samuel 21–26. Then review the questions below concerning this section of 1–2 Samuel and write your notes on them. (For further background, see the *ESV Study Bible*, pages 526–534; available online at esv.org.)

1. The King on the Run (chs. 21–22)

Some have wondered whether David's actions in Nob are biblically permissible, since only priests are to eat the holy bread (Lev. 24:9). However, Jesus comments on this very scene. Read Mark 2:23–28. How does Jesus' commentary affect our understanding of David's receiving the holy bread?

In recent chapters, David has more than once "fled" the scene because of Saul's threats (1 Sam. 19:10, 18; 20:1, 42). Now in 21:10 he flees to Gath. Look back to 1 Samuel 17:4 to recall the significance of this town. How desperate must David be to flee from Saul to Gath? Do you think David is sinfully distrusting the Lord when he feigns insanity before the king of Gath (21:13)? Read Psalm 56 (written by David about his capture in Gath) and Psalm 34 (written about his feigned insanity and escape). How do these psalms help us to understand the scene in Gath?

In 22:1 David flees again, now to a cave in the wilderness. This once again shows how desperate and alone he truly is (see Psalm 142). But he is soon joined by family (1 Sam. 22:1), then by 400 others (v. 2). How are these 400 described, and what significance might this have for understanding the differing leadership styles of Saul and David?

Sandwiched between scenes in the cave with David and his men (22:1–5, 20–23) is a horrific scene of Saul's brutal execution of the priests of Nob and their families via his henchman, Doeg the Edomite (vv. 16–19). This provides an important contrast between the two "kings." What contrasts do you see between Saul and David in chapter 22?

Echoes from earlier in 1 Samuel ring out in chapter 22 (perhaps foremost is 15:18–19). In what ways can you compare and contrast these stories?

---

2. The King Who Saves and Is Saved (ch. 23)

The contrasts between these two "kings" will become even starker as this book progresses. How do David's actions in 23:1–5 add further contrast to the results of Saul's leadership in the previous chapter?

One major contrast between Saul and David is that the latter seeks and hears from God. Where exactly in chapter 23 do we see David's seeking and hearing from the Lord, and what difference does this make in chapters 22–23?

The people of Keilah are saved from the threat of the Philistines by David and his men, only to turn against David soon thereafter (23:8, 12). This is sad, indeed, but is it terribly surprising? How might John 1:11 speak to this reality?

----

3. The King Who Spares (chs. 24–26)

Twice David has had opportunity to take Saul's life, but each time he has refused (24:1–15; 26:7–20). What reasons does David provide for sparing Saul? See specifically 24:6, 10, 12; 26:9–11, 23–24.

Between two scenes of David's sparing Saul, we read of another life spared under quite different circumstances (ch. 25). David initially plans to wipe out Nabal for refusing to extend the most basic cultural norms of hospitality. However, Abigail pleads with David on account of God's royal promises to him (vv. 26–31). The future king happily relents, and justice is once again entrusted to the Lord.

What else do we learn about David from this rather peculiar chapter, especially in light of its position in this three-story-sandwich of chapters 24–26?

Saul expresses a kind of remorse in each of his close encounters with David (24:16–21; 26:21–25). Reading on, we soon realize that it is not genuine repentance that Saul expresses. However, he does make a request that David takes seriously and later honors. What is it?

Read through the following three sections on *Gospel Glimpses*, *Whole-Bible Connections*, and *Theological Soundings*. Then take time to consider the *Personal Implications* these sections may have for you.

Gospel Glimpses

THE LOWLY AND NEEDY. Those who join David at the cave of Adullam are people "in distress, . . . in debt, and . . . bitter in soul" (1 Sam. 22:2). It is not explicit in the text, but in context it seems likely that these are people disenfranchised and disillusioned by Saul's kingship. Samuel warned the people that the kind of king they sought ("a king like the nations") would *take and take and take* for himself (8:11–17). In contrast, David is a king who welcomes the lowly and needy. Such people find refuge in him. This trait is, of course, found in a later king as well: Jesus, a "friend of tax collectors and sinners" (Luke 7:34) who announced, "Come to me, all who labor and are heavy laden, and I will give you rest" (Matt. 11:28).

SAFETY AND THREAT. In the eyes of many, it would seem wiser and safer to be in Saul's company as he sits regally under a tamarisk tree with soldiers arrayed about (1 Sam. 22:6) than to join the hunted David in the wilderness. In fact, David grieves that the gruesome massacre of a whole priestly city resulted, in part, from his visit with Ahimelech (v. 22). But it is just then that David utters these curious words: "Stay with me; do not be afraid, for he who seeks my life seeks your life. With me you shall be in safekeeping" (22:23). Is it safe to be with David? Yes and no. He is "public enemy number one," with a whole army on his tail. But he is also truly the Lord's anointed. The Lord is with him, so to be with him is about as safe as it gets. And so it is with Jesus. We flee to the true King even though he does not look like a king, and even when it does not seem safe to identify with him. Paradoxically, Jesus promised, "You will be delivered up even by parents and brothers and relatives and friends, and some of you they will put to death. . . . *But not a hair of your head will perish*" (Luke 21:16–18). Even through betrayal and death, God is sovereignly watching over the very hairs of our head. If we are with Jesus, we are safe, no matter what (see Rom. 8:31–39).

Whole-Bible Connections

HELP FROM THE PSALMS. Roughly a dozen psalms can be tied to specific events in 1–2 Samuel. Such psalms not only provide a personal, experiential window into events in 1–2 Samuel but also can help us to interpret such events. This is certainly the case with 1 Samuel 21 and its related psalms, Psalms 34 and 56. Why does David flee to Philistine land? These psalms make clear that the circumstances are just that desperate—and desperate times call for desperate measures. Though he is afraid (Ps. 56:3), David clearly puts his trust in the Lord (vv. 4ff.). Likewise, it may be tempting to assess David's feigned insanity as a lack of faith, but Psalm 34 makes clear that David sees his escape as nothing less than an answer to prayer and the Lord's rescue. Therefore, the lesson from Gath is that the Lord does not always save with sword or spear; he may even use *spittle* (1 Sam. 21:13) to prove that he works in surprising, seemingly upside-down ways. Is the cross not the epitome of this truth? Read 1 Corinthians 1:18–31 for a reminder.

Theological Soundings

SIN'S BEWILDERING EFFECTS. Saul's downward spiral is instructive for us. Sin creates a vortex, always taking us deeper than we want or plan to go. Recall that early on, Saul appeared as a man with potential but also weakness. At first, his self-focus and fears seemed fairly harmless—remember his hiding at his inauguration (1 Sam. 10:22)? Soon, however, Saul's rebellious self-centeredness manifests itself more blatantly (chs. 13–15). Not long after this, his appreciation for David's successes turns to jealousy, then murderous tantrums (ch. 18). He conspires against David in the most duplicitous of ways (chs. 18–19). By chapter 22 Saul fully occupies himself and his whole army with a relentless manhunt. Surely one of the darkest moments is the gruesome execution of every living creature in Nob. Remember how Saul once refused to obey God's command to obliterate the wicked Amalekites (ch. 15)? Now he holds nothing back against his own priests, simply because one of them has aided David. Saul's close encounters with David (chs. 24; 26) show a man riddled with guilt but ultimately unrepentant. And this downward spiral is not finished! So let us be warned. As with many characters and events in the Old Testament, this statement is true of Saul as well: "These things took place as examples for us, that we might not desire evil as they did. . . . Therefore let anyone who thinks that he stands take heed lest he fall" (1 Cor. 10:6, 12).

DAVID'S IMPEFRECT RIGHTEOUSNESS. We should keep noting the contrast between Saul and David—one man sinful and going further astray; the other man righteous and reliant on the Lord—but a subtler matter should also be noted. David is righteous, but he is not perfect. He can at times fly off the handle and head out for needless conflict (1 Sam. 25:13, 34). Thankfully, in God's providence,[1] Abigail steps in, and David relents. But no sooner is that crisis avoided than a new one subtly creeps into the picture: by the end of chapter 25, David has multiple wives. We are not explicitly told here that this is sin. But we should recall a passage that David surely knew, one in which God warned Israel's future king, "He shall not acquire many wives for himself" (Deut. 17:17). So both his quick temper against Nabal and his multiple wives remind us subtly that David is a good king but far from a perfect one. But praise God that the final son of David, the true King, is not merely perfectly righteous, but perfectly righteous *on our behalf* (2 Cor. 5:21).

> ## Personal Implications

Take time to reflect on the implications of 1 Samuel 21–26 for your own life today. Consider what you have learned that might lead you to praise God, repent of sin, and trust more deeply in his gracious promises. Write down your reflections under the three headings we have considered and on the passage as a whole.

1. Gospel Glimpses

2. Whole-Bible Connections

_____

_____

_____

_____

_____

3. Theological Soundings

_____

_____

_____

_____

_____

4. 1 Samuel 21–26

_____

_____

_____

_____

_____

_____

▶ As You Finish This Unit . . .

Take a moment now to ask for the Lord's blessing and help as you continue in this study of 1–2 Samuel. And take a moment also to look back through this unit of study, to reflect on some key things that the Lord may be teaching you.

Definition

[1] **Providence** – God's good, wise, and sovereign guidance and control of all things, by which he supplies all our needs and accomplishes his holy will.

Week 7: Saul's Undoing, David's Deliverance

1 Samuel 27–2 Samuel 1

▲

The Place of the Passage

Desperation leads David into Philistine land once again, but this time compromises (1 Sam. 27:8–12) lead to multiplied complications. Nevertheless, God sovereignly intervenes, protecting his anointed from greater sin (ch. 29). Meanwhile, Saul's doubts and fears lead to deeper depths of darkness. Desperate for supernatural insight, he turns to a medium, a witch (ch. 28), only to receive another confirming word of his impending doom. The author turns attention repeatedly back and forth between David and Saul in order to highlight further a contrast of two "kings," one on a trajectory toward the throne (which plays out in 2 Samuel) and the other spiraling off of the throne in spectacular disgrace (which ends in 1 Samuel 31). This is the outworking of God's promises made long ago (e.g., 1 Sam. 2:10; 13:13–14; 15:28; 16:13).

The Big Picture

Saul's life and kingship come to a prophesied disgraceful end because of his grave sin; David is protected from himself and his enemies because God's hand rests upon him.

Reflection and Discussion

Read through the complete passage for this study, 1 Samuel 27–2 Samuel 1. Then review the questions below concerning this section of 1–2 Samuel and write your notes on them. (For further background, see the *ESV Study Bible*, pages 535–544; available online at esv.org.)

1. David Flees to the Philistines (1 Samuel 27, 29)

The knot of issues in 1 Samuel 27 is notoriously difficult to untie. For example, how severely does David's faith falter? Which of his actions are sinful, and which are desperately shrewd? To appreciate the complexities, list both positive and negative observations concerning David's actions, looking for clues in the text itself.

It had been David's regular practice to seek the Lord's guidance (e.g., 23:2, 4) and to refer to the Lord in conversation (25:34; 26:10). Do we see the same in chapters 27–29? What might this answer suggest?

We come to a crucial crossroads at 28:1–2. Keeping the circumstances of chapter 27 in mind, list potential complexities that might be on the horizon.

How are these complexities averted in chapter 29? Who is responsible for this outcome?

----

2. Saul Finds a Witch in Endor (1 Samuel 28)

Saul consults a necromancer (someone who seeks to communicate with the dead) in chapter 28. What circumstances lead him to do this, according to the text? What is he hoping to gain from this encounter? What should he have done instead?

A number of sad ironies can be noted on the final night of Saul's life (28:15–25). List a few.

----

3. David Is Restored and Rescues Captives (1 Samuel 30)

While a crisis seems to be averted in chapter 29, the next chapter introduces another crisis occurring elsewhere (30:1–5). This crisis reaches a boiling point in verse 6a, but in verse 6b there is a turn in the right direction. What is this turn, and what is its significance, in light of the last few chapters?

Both Saul and David are "strengthened" in a moment of crisis (28:22–25; 30:6), but quite differently. How so?

In 30:21–22 we see a controversy over spoils taken from the Amalekites. How does David handle this controversy (vv. 23–31), and what do these actions communicate about his leadership?

4. Saul's Death and David's Lament (1 Samuel 31–2 Samuel 1)

Saul's death is recorded in 1 Samuel 31. A slightly different version is told by an Amalekite in 2 Samuel 1. How do we explain these discrepancies? What do you think the Amalekite's intentions are?

Though already dead, Saul is decapitated by the Philistines (31:9). Two other figures are also decapitated in 1 Samuel (see 5:4; 17:51). Do you think this is mere coincidence? If not, what is the significance of this similarity? What do these three figures have in common?

It is unsurprising that David mourns the death of his friend Jonathan, but it may be surprising that he also mourns Saul's death. Why do you think David laments the death of Saul?

This pivotal moment is a good time to look back again to Hannah's prayer (1 Sam. 2:1–10). What foreshadowings and promises in her prayer are realized in the chapters studied this week?

Read through the following three sections on *Gospel Glimpses*, *Whole-Bible Connections*, and *Theological Soundings*. Then take time to consider the *Personal Implications* these sections may have for you.

Gospel Glimpses

GOD OVERCOMES WEAKNESS. David's time in Philistia (1 Samuel 27, 29) seems to be a season of faltering faith. David does not seek the Lord; in fact, the only mentions of the Lord at all in these chapters are on the lips of the pagan king Achish (29:6, 9)! Indeed, David's words at the outset seem to betray a measure of spiritual weakness: "David said in his heart, 'Now I shall *perish* one day by the hand of Saul'" (27:1). On one level, this is proper skepticism that Saul's promise to relent (26:21) would be kept. On another level, David is calling into question his very anointing (ch. 16). He is doubting God's promises, which have been recounted to him recently by Jonathan (23:17), Abigail (25:28–31), and even Saul (24:20; 26:25). Doubt leads David to Philistia, leading to compromise and lies, followed by a collision course with Israel's army (28:1–2). It seems like a no-win situation—until God intervenes (29:4–7). Of course, we are not told explicitly that God intervenes. But there is no need for the narrator to restate the obvious. God is intervening in David's life to protect him as promised (2:9–10), this time from the consequences of his own weakness and sin. Praise God, he does this for all of his people (Rom. 8:28). This does not mean that our sin will never have consequences. But it is true, and proven over and over, that "He does not deal with us according to our sins" (Ps. 103:10). Reflect on times in which God has turned your foolishness around or protected you from yourself.

Whole-Bible Connections

HEARING FROM GOD. It is a very good thing when God speaks (1 Sam. 3:1, 21). Through Saul we have a window into the inverse: God's judgment through eerie silence. Saul is desperate to hear something from the Lord, but he receives silence (28:6)—only to hear the silence broken by a fresh pronouncement of judgment (28:15ff.). This should remind us of a time much later, when God is silent for 400 years following the final Old Testament prophet. One prophet foretold, "'Behold, the days are coming,' declares the Lord GOD, 'when I will send a famine on the land—not a famine of bread, nor a thirst for water, but of hearing the words of the LORD'" (Amos 8:11). After 400 long years, this silence was broken: "The Word became flesh and dwelt among us, and we have seen his glory, glory as of the only Son from the Father, full of grace and truth" (John 1:14). God has spoken uniquely in his Son, the heir and creator of all (Heb. 1:2). And, praise God, he still speaks today through his living and active Word, the Holy Scriptures (Heb. 4:12).

DECISION MAKING. In 1 Samuel 27–30, enquiring of the Lord is done primarily for guidance concerning issues related mostly to warfare (23:2; 28:6; 30:8). The answers come in a variety of ways: dreams, prophets, or the Urim and Thummim (see 1 Sam. 14:41). And sometimes they do not come at all (28:6). Decision making in the Bible is often more complicated than flipping a coin or waiting for a voice from heaven. For instance, in Acts, Paul sometimes received a special word of guidance (Acts 9:6; 13:2; 16:7–9); however, many other times he or others simply "decided" (Acts 20:3), "resolved" (Acts 19:21), or concluded that an option "seemed good" (Acts 15:22, 34 [see ESV footnote]). We cannot expect God always to provide us with miraculous guidance. We must always ask if Scripture commands or forbids a potential course of action. We should also seek godly counsel (Prov. 11:14), pray for open doors (Col. 4:3), and remember to pray, "Your kingdom come, your will be done" (Matt. 6:10).

Theological Soundings

BEHOLD, KINDNESS AND SEVERITY. Our God is astoundingly merciful and kind. He is also fearfully holy and just. The apostle Paul tells us to "note then the kindness and the severity of God: severity toward those who have fallen, but God's kindness to you, provided you continue in his kindness. Otherwise you too will be cut off" (Rom. 11:22). We are to *note*—take notice, behold, apprehend, marvel at—God's mercy and his judgment. The books of Samuel are full of examples of mercy and judgment, not least in the chapters studied this week. Let us take note of God's manifold kindnesses to David; let us note carefully his undeterred, righteous judgments against Saul. Let us not presume upon his grace; and let us not think that our sin is too great for him to overcome. Indeed, in the words of Paul, may we "continue in his kindness" by beholding his "kindness and . . . severity."

SEEKING THE LORD. As a "man after [God's] own heart" (1 Sam. 13:14), David seeks the Lord for more than guidance, as his many psalms demonstrate powerfully. Saul seeks the Lord in a very different way. When we are told that Saul "inquired of the LORD, [but] the LORD did not answer him" (28:6), we should not assume that Saul has sought the Lord genuinely. With an increasingly seared conscience,[1] Saul seeks inside information only to benefit himself. And when the Lord will not give him what he wants, he is willing to turn anywhere for it (v. 7). There is a big difference between seeking the Lord himself and seeking only what he can give in order to serve ourselves.

> ## Personal Implications

Take time to reflect on the implications of 1 Samuel 27–2 Samuel 1 for your own life today. Consider what you have learned that might lead you to praise God, repent of sin, and trust more deeply in his gracious promises. Write down your reflections under the three headings we have considered and on the passage as a whole.

1. Gospel Glimpses

2. Whole-Bible Connections

3. Theological Soundings

---

4. 1 Samuel 27–2 Samuel 1

> ## As You Finish This Unit . . .

Take a moment now to ask for the Lord's blessing and help as you continue in this study of 1–2 Samuel. And take a moment also to look back through this unit of study, to reflect on some key things that the Lord may be teaching you.

Definition

[1] **Conscience** – The ability to understand the rightness or wrongness of one's actions and motives. One's conscience is not identical to the inner witness of the Holy Spirit, for the conscience is subject to the corruption of sin, although the Holy Spirit often employs a redeemed conscience in guiding people and convicting them of sin.

Week 8: David's Kingdom Established and Ensured

2 Samuel 2–10

▲

The Place of the Passage

Following the death of Saul, David is anointed king by the tribe of Judah. The other 11 tribes initially oppose David (2 Samuel 3–4) before finally joining Judah under his kingship (ch. 5). Now the dominoes of blessing begin to fall on God's people under David's godly, unifying leadership, with Jerusalem as his new capital. Worship is restored (ch. 6), promises are enlarged (ch. 7), enemies are defeated (chs. 5, 8, 10), and old promises are kept (ch. 9). Chapters 5 to 10 are among the most celebratory portions of all of 1–2 Samuel. But we are once again left wondering how long this high point will last. The subsequent chapters will tell us, as David will sin greatly (ch. 11) and suffer for it severely (chs. 12–19). Yet, despite David's sin and its consequences, God's kingdom will prevail, because his promises are sure.

The Big Picture

When all of Israel recognizes David as its rightful king, God brings spectacular blessing to his people by means of his anointed—a man after God's own heart, a man of his choosing.

> ## Reflection and Discussion

Read through the complete passage for this study, 2 Samuel 2–10. Then review the questions below concerning this section of 1–2 Samuel and write your notes on them. (For further background, see the *ESV Study Bible*, pages 544–559; available online at esv.org.)

1. A Contested King (chs. 2–4)

Besides the death of Saul, what is the impetus for David's going up to Hebron, in the land of Judah? Put another way, what does he do before going to Hebron?

What are David's intentions or hopes in sending a word of blessing to the men of Jabesh-gilead (2:5–7)?

The events, characters, and issues of chapters 2–4 can be difficult to follow. But a convenient summary is provided in 3:1. In what ways do the events described in 3:1 play out more specifically in chapters 2–4?

2. A Celebrated King (chs. 5–7)

When the tribes of Israel finally recognize David as their king (5:1–3), what reasons do they give for doing so? In the grand scheme of 1–2 Samuel, what significance do their reasons have?

According to chapter 5, why is David so successful in his early endeavors as king?

Chapter 6 relates an incident involving the ark, continuing and contrasting an earlier ark narrative (1 Sam. 5:1–7:2). What are some similarities between the two ark-related stories? What are some important contrasts?

Considering the instructions God had given for handling the ark (Num. 4:1–20), what does Uzzah do wrong in 2 Samuel 6? Why is he judged so severely?

A play on words is evident in 2 Samuel 7, involving the word "house." David intends to build the Lord a "house," but God insists that he will build David a different kind of "house" (vv. 1–13). Explain what this means.

David has received various royal promises and assurances in his life thus far (see 1 Sam. 16:13; 23:17; 24:20; 25:28–30; 2 Sam. 2:4; 5:1–3); however, 2 Samuel 7 enlarges these promises for David and his throne. How so?

How does David respond to the Lord's alternative "house" plans (see 7:18–29)? What does this say about the kind of king we are reading about?

3. A Conquering King (chs. 8; 10)

Chapters 8 and 10 highlight David's great military successes. In light of earlier land-related promises and military commissions (e.g., Gen. 15:18–21; Deut. 9:3–5; 20:10–18), what is the significance of David's victories here?

How do David's victories (and general leadership) affect Israel in 1 Samuel 8 and 10? Point to specific verses and language.

4. A Compassionate King (ch. 9)

How does David's kindness to Mephibosheth relate to previous passages in 1–2 Samuel? (See especially 1 Sam. 20:13–17; 24:20–22; 2 Sam. 4:4.)

How does the Mephibosheth narrative compare or contrast to the stories in its immediate context (2 Samuel 8 and 10)?

Does anything in Hannah's prayer (1 Sam. 2:1–10) reverberate in the Mephibosheth story (2 Samuel 9)? What specifically?

How might Saul's reign, on the whole, compare or contrast to David's reign as described in 2 Samuel 8–10?

Read through the following three sections on *Gospel Glimpses*, *Whole-Bible Connections*, and *Theological Soundings*. Then take time to consider the *Personal Implications* these sections may have for you.

Gospel Glimpses

COVENANT KEEPING KINDNESS. David shows remarkable kindness to Mephiboseth because he had long ago made a covenant with his friend Jonathan to show "steadfast love" to Jonathan's family (1 Sam. 20:15–16). David is a covenant keeping king, relentlessly so. Mephibosheth has nothing to offer the king. Indeed, he is not only crippled (2 Sam. 4:4; 9:3) but he is also the descendant of Saul. Kings in these days would regularly eliminate whole families who could possibly lay claim to the throne. Mephibosheth, humanly speaking, has every reason to fear a summons to the king. But, as we have seen, David is not like most kings. He assures Mephibosheth, "Do not fear, for I will show you *kindness* for the sake of your father Jonathan" (9:7). The Hebrew word for kindness here is *hesed*, referring most often in Scripture to God's covenantal affection, care, and commitment to his people (often translated "steadfast love" in the ESV). It is not accidental or coincidental that David uses that word for his kindness to Mephibosheth. He earlier pledged to show Saul's lineage "the kindness [*hesed*] of God" (9:3). David's attitude and actions toward Mephibosheth flow from the character of God and David's experience with that kind, covenant keeping God. This same God of *hesed* has shown covenantal kindness in Christ to all who come to him in faith. While "we were still weak . . . Christ died for us" (Rom 5:6–8); in fact, worse then weak, we were Christ's "enemies" (Rom. 5:10). We had nothing to offer. There was no reason for God to show us kindness—but he did so anyway, for Jesus' sake. And now we are no longer his enemies but his sons and daughters. He sups with us in Communion,[1] and one day we will dine with him forever (Rev. 19:9). The Mephibosheth story is a wonderful foreshadow of these realities.

Whole-Bible Connections

HEBRON. "Go up . . . to Hebron," God directed David (2 Sam. 2:1), and there David is made king of Judah. Hebron is a place with rich history. It is where God granted Abram promises for innumerable offspring, a land, a nation, and a blessing that would reach the ends of the earth (Genesis 15; 17). God also promised Abraham that, through his wife, Sarah, "kings of peoples" and "nations" would come from him (17:16). Now, almost a thousand years later, David is anointed as king in Hebron. It is something of a new beginning, but one very much in continuity with and building upon the promises of old.

OLD KINGLY PROMISES. Not only was Abraham told that kings would come from him, but his great-grandson Judah also received a more elaborate promise of a ruler to come: "The scepter shall not depart from Judah, . . . and to him shall be the obedience of the peoples" (Gen. 49:10). Yet in the days of the judges, a mournful chorus arose: "In those days there was *no king* in Israel. Everyone did what was right in his own eyes" (Judg. 17:6; 21:25). But then 1 Samuel began with a renewed hope for a *king*, God's *anointed* (2:10). By now in 1–2 Samuel, it is clear that David is that king. Or is he? Is he really adequate to fulfill the grand royal promises given to Abraham and Judah? And what if the promises become even grander? See below.

THE DAVIDIC COVENANT. God's promises to David in 2 Samuel 7 have near and far implications. Many of these promises are specific to David's son Solomon—he will build a "house" (temple) for the Lord (v. 13). Other promises reach into eternity. Indeed, three times God assures David of an *eternal* Davidic throne (vv. 13, 16). David's interpretation of these promises is further enlightening. In his prayer of response he thanks God for (literally, in the Hebrew) a *charter for mankind* (v. 19). Yet, God also hints at David's death (v. 12) and at the sins of the Davidic line (v. 14). These realities reach significant tension in the years of the prophets, when many Davidic kings go astray (and die), and even more so when there is no Davidic king on the throne at all (see Psalm 89). But such tensions begin to see resolution when the New Testament begins: "The genealogy of Jesus Christ [Anointed/Messiah], *the son of David*, the son of Abraham" (Matt. 1:1). Jesus alone can fulfill the *eternal* Davidic kingly promises. We see how important this is from other portions of the New Testament: e.g., Luke 1:32–33; Acts 2:29–31; 13:34–39; 15:16–17; 2 Timothy 2:8; Revelation 5:5.

Theological Soundings

GOD'S TIMING. Let us put ourselves in David's shoes. He was first anointed as king-in-waiting back in 1 Samuel 16, probably in his mid-teen years. Would we have expected the long, winding, and terribly trying road to the throne? For many years David was anointed but on the run and in constant danger. God was with him, but on the surface quite the opposite would often appear to be true. But David *walked by faith, not by sight*, remarkably well. Even after Saul's death—perhaps 20 years after his anointing—when only one tribe recognizes his rightful reign, David still does not take the other tribes by force (2 Samuel 2–4). We can learn a lot from David (see Rom. 15:4). God's promises are sure, even though the timing is his own and the path he takes us on may be surprising or difficult.

Personal Implications

Take time to reflect on the implications of 2 Samuel 2–10 for your own life today. Consider what you have learned that might lead you to praise God, repent of sin,

and trust more deeply in his gracious promises. Write down your reflections under the three headings we have considered and on the passage as a whole.

1. Gospel Glimpses

_____

_____

_____

_____

_____

2. Whole-Bible Connections

_____

_____

_____

_____

_____

3. Theological Soundings

_____

_____

_____

_____

_____

4. 2 Samuel 2–10

_____

_____

_____

_____

As You Finish This Unit . . .

Take a moment now to ask for the Lord's blessing and help as you continue in this study of 1–2 Samuel. And take a moment also to look back through this unit of study, to reflect on some key things that the Lord may be teaching you.

Definition

[1] **Communion** – The fellowship and unity that all believers share as a result of the work of the Holy Spirit in their hearts. Such communion among believers can be expressed in various ways, including worshiping God together, sharing possessions and resources, and partaking of the Lord's Supper, which has come to be referred to also as Communion.

WEEK 9: DAVID'S GREAT SIN AND ITS CONSEQUENCES

2 Samuel 11–14

▲

The author/editor of 2 Samuel has rightly raised the reader's expectations for David's kingdom through the lofty, celebratory chapters of 2 Samuel 1–10. However, considering David's multiplying sins of 2 Samuel 11, and the consequences that ripple through the rest of 2 Samuel, we might wonder if this once-promising kingdom will come crashing down. But we should recall words from the Davidic covenant: "When he commits iniquity, I will discipline him . . . but my steadfast love will not depart from him, as I took it from Saul. . . . Your throne will be established forever" (2 Sam. 7:14–16). David's sin will not undo God's promises. And yet, there is no escaping the fact that these are some of the darkest chapters of the entire Bible.

The Big Picture

David spirals into sin and deception; when confronted, he confesses and receives forgiveness, but not without severe consequences.

> ### Reflection and Discussion

Read through the complete passage for this study, 2 Samuel 11–14. Then review the questions below concerning this section of 1–2 Samuel and write your notes on them. (For further background, see the *ESV Study Bible*, pages 559–566; available online at esv.org.)

1. Sin: David, Bathsheba, and Uriah (ch. 11)

What might the author be subtly suggesting by the way in which he sets the stage for this passage in 11:1–2a?

On whom does the text lay blame (or primary blame) for this adulterous affair (vv. 1–4)? Be suspicious of what you may have heard or imagined, and let the text speak for itself.

How many cover-up schemes does David attempt (vv. 6–25)? Do you see any pattern or trajectory to these attempts? If so, what does this fact indicate?

Compare David's words of assurance to Joab (v. 25) with the editorial comment about God's perspective (v. 27). How do these statements differ, and what does this difference communicate to the reader?

Recall the contrast between Israel's ideal king (Deut. 17:16–20) and typical kings of the nations (1 Sam. 8:10–17). Which kind of king is David acting like in 2 Samuel 11? Provide specifics.

---

2. Repentance: Nathan, David, and the Child (ch. 12)

Why does the prophet Nathan begin his confrontation of David with an allegory[1] (12:1–4)? How does this approach serve to bring about David's conviction of his guilt (see vv. 5–9)?

Verse 13 contains David's brief but genuine confession. However, Psalm 51 was written as a prayer of confession for this very sin. What in Psalm 51 stands out as particularly apropos of the events of 2 Samuel 11–12?

This chapter demonstrates an important principle in the difference between judicial punishment of sin and real-life consequences of sin, between God's mercy and his discipline (see 7:14–15). What consequences are spelled out by the prophet (12:10–14)? What connection might these specific consequences have to the sins of chapter 11?

How does David respond to the Lord's discipline in 12:15–23? What do these verses communicate about David's present relationship with the Lord?

3. Consequences: Amnon, Tamar, and Absalom (ch. 13–14)

While Amnon's rape of his sister is exceptionally, breathtakingly wicked, there are some parallels between this sin and David's sins in chapter 11. What are they?

Read Galatians 6:7 and Hebrews 12:5–11. How do these texts apply to 2 Samuel 13–14?

What is David's reaction to hearing of Tamar's rape (see 2 Sam. 13:21–23)? What is missing? How does 1 Kings 1:6 illuminate a broader issue at work here?

How is David's passivity further demonstrated in 2 Samuel 13:34–14:33? What added complications arise as a result?

It may appear that there is reconciliation between father and son at the end of chapter 14, but subtle clues in verses 32–33 indicate otherwise. What are they?

Read through the following three sections on *Gospel Glimpses*, *Whole-Bible Connections*, and *Theological Soundings*. Then take time to consider the *Personal Implications* these sections may have for you.

Gospel Glimpses

CONFRONTATION. As a prophet, Nathan had a unique responsibility to confront David's sin—indeed, he was sent by the Lord (2 Sam. 12:1) and was presumably given divine insight into the king's sin. This was a unique situation, not one we are to imitate in every way. That said, confrontation of sin should not be a completely foreign concept to New Testament believers. Especially in the context of a local church, we have been called to confront gently but firmly when we see a brother or sister go astray (see Matt. 7:4; 18:15–20; Gal. 6:1; 2 Tim. 2:24–26; James 5:19–20). And we have been called to receive correction when needed. It is not easy to give or receive correction. But this is part of God's plan for our spiritual safety and sanctification. We are not prophets like Nathan, but he is a reminder of how important others are in our fight against sin.

CLEANSING. It is important to note carefully the extent (brazenness, depth, persistence, callousness, etc.) of David's sins. Only then will we rightly be astonished at the prophet's words, "The LORD also has put away your sin" (2 Sam. 12:13). And this follows the briefest of confessions (v. 13). Of course, as mentioned above, Psalm 51 fills out what is in David's heart and mind when he confesses. In that psalm David speaks at length about the depth and darkness of his sins (vv. 3–6). He also expresses faith in God's covenantal mercies, his character, and his ability to blot out those sins (vv. 1–2, 6–12). It is astounding: What great sin! What greater grace!

Whole-Bible Connections

CLEANSING, BUT HOW? While the prophet's assurance, "The LORD also has put away your sin," is wonderful news for sinners (2 Sam. 12:13), and while David's confidence in God's ability to cleanse sinners completely is a hopeful model, it raises the question of how this is possible. How does God *blot out* and *wash away* sin (Ps. 51:1–2)? Where does sin go? How does the Lord simply *put it away*? The New Testament makes it clear that this act was not simple at all. In Romans we read, "All have sinned and fall short of the glory of God, and are justified by his grace as a gift, *through the redemption that is in Christ Jesus*, whom *God put forward as a propitiation by his blood*, to be received by faith. This was to show God's righteousness, . . . so that he might be *just* and *the justifier* of the one who has faith in Jesus" (Rom. 3:23–26). The sins of Old Testament saints awaited the payment that would come with Christ. On the cross, the payment for his people's sin was made in full once for all. With this understanding we can receive the joyous news, "The LORD has put away your sin," and pray with even greater confidence, "Wash me, and I shall be whiter than snow" (Ps. 51:7). Ironically, we are washed white "in the blood of the Lamb" (Rev. 7:14).

Theological Soundings

TYPE AND NEGATIVE TYPE. We have seen that God's promises to and blessings through David were foreshadowings of the greater King, Jesus, and his kingdom. Yet we have seen also that the promises given to David were far too grand for him to experience fully—e.g., promises that God would establish an eternal throne, even though David himself would eventually "lie down" and die (2 Sam. 7:12). Further, we have seen *ups* and *downs* in the life of David. When God's promises seem to be fulfilled and the plan seems to advance (the *ups*), David functions as a *type*[2] of the coming Christ. However, when David sins greatly and the kingdom is affected severely, David functions as an *negative type* of the true Christ. As the former (*type*), David provides a remarkable, hope-giving preview of God's kingdom under the godly rule of his anointed king (see 2 Sam. 8:15). As the latter (*negative type*), David provides a painful but necessary reminder that another, better king is still desperately needed. We must have a place for each type in our theology as we read through Old Testament narrative. It could not be any clearer what 2 Samuel 11–14 teaches us: this sinful David is not the one. A greater, more righteous king is still needed. Or, from our vantage point, we can recognize Jesus *as* that righteous One (Luke 7:20–22)—we do not wait for another. Instead, we wait only for him to come again (1 Thess. 4:16–17)!

▶ Personal Implications

Take time to reflect on the implications of 2 Samuel 11–14 for your own life today. Consider what you have learned that might lead you to praise God, repent of sin, and trust more deeply in his gracious promises. Write down your reflections under the three headings we have considered and on the passage as a whole.

1. Gospel Glimpses

2. Whole-Bible Connections

3. Theological Soundings

4. 2 Samuel 11–14

> ## As You Finish This Unit . . .

Take a moment now to ask for the Lord's blessing and help as you continue in this study of 1–2 Samuel. And take a moment also to look back through this unit of study, to reflect on some key things that the Lord may be teaching you.

Definitions

[1] **Allegory** – A story that communicates truth through a symbolic understanding of its literal meaning. In allegory characters, objects, and actions specifically represent things in a parallel spiritual or moral context.

[2] **Type** – A real, historical object, place, or person recognized as a pattern or foreshadow of some later object, place, or person. For example, the Bible presents Adam and David as types of Christ (see Acts 2:24–28; Rom. 5:14). The fulfillment of a type (in this case, Christ) is known as an *antitype* (that is, the "antitype," for the sake of comparison, is placed over against [anti-] the type).

WEEK 10: ABSALOM'S REBELLION, DAVID'S RESTORATION

2 Samuel 15–20

The Place of the Passage

David's grave sins were forgiven, but painful consequences remained: the death of a child (2 Samuel 12), then violence among David's children (chs. 13–14), and now a coup and civil war led by his son Absalom (chs. 15–18). David is once again a king on the run and in great danger. As promised, God will continue to *give strength to his king and exalt his anointed* (1 Sam. 2:10)—Absalom will perish (2 Samuel 18) and David's reign will be restored (ch. 19)—but not without ongoing pockets of strife and grief (ch. 20).

The Big Picture

God's promises for an enduring (eternal) Davidic kingdom are sure and unchanging, but the kingdom looks to be hanging by a thread throughout Absalom's coup and its aftermath.

> ### Reflection and Discussion

Read through the complete passage for this study, 2 Samuel 15–20. Then review the questions below concerning this section of 1–2 Samuel and write your notes on them. (For further background, see the *ESV Study Bible*, pages 566–576 available online at esv.org.)

1. Absalom's Coup (ch. 15)

In what ways does Absalom conspire against his father, according to 15:1–12?

While chapter 15 does not lay blame on David for Absalom's rebellion, how do previous chapters (chs. 12–14) place a measure of responsibility on David for these events?

Psalm 3 was written by David as he lamented Absalom's revolt. What in Psalm 3 stands out as particularly illuminating for 2 Samuel 15ff.? What does Psalm 3 tell us about (a) David's sorrows and (b) his faith?

----

2. Other Opponents (chs. 16–17)

While there are dozens of names in chapters 16–17, five or six characters especially relate to David in some significant way. Who are they, and how does each relate to David?

What is the significance of Absalom's taking David's concubines (16:21–23)? Consider the significance *morally*, *politically*, and *biblically* (see 12:11–12).

3. Absalom's Death (ch. 18)

David tells his army leaders to "Deal gently for my sake with the young man Absalom" (18:5). How do you understand David here: as a father rightly caring for his son, or as a weak king whose sentimentality overrides prudence and justice? Why?

According to 18:9, how is Absalom apprehended before his death? How might 14:26 further explain what happens in the tree on that fateful day? How might the frequent use of irony in 1–2 Samuel factor into these verses?

What should we make of David's grief over Absalom's death? (While a definitive answer may not be obvious, some clues might be discerned from 18:31–33.)

---

4. David's Return (chs. 19–20)

With Absalom dead and David back in Jerusalem, there is a necessary reckoning for those who joined the opposition against the true king. In 19:11–43 there is one kind of reckoning, while in 20:1–22 there is another. How do they differ? How does each reflect an aspect of the kingdom of God?[1]

Read Psalm 2. How do the tensions and promises of Psalm 2 play out in 2 Samuel 15–20?

How have the foreshadowings in Hannah's song (1 Sam. 2:1–10) come to light in 2 Samuel 15–20?

Read through the following three sections on *Gospel Glimpses, Whole-Bible Connections*, and *Theological Soundings*. Then take time to consider the *Personal Implications* these sections may have for you.

Gospel Glimpses

HOLDING ON TO PROMISES. There is very little "gospel" (good news) in these chapters. However, these chapters do teach us more than just the darkness of sin. They also underscore the surety of God's promises—promises of *difficulty and discipline*, as well as of *strength and salvation*. God promised to discipline his son (2 Sam. 7:14–15; 12:9–14), and 2 Samuel 15–20 portrays just that. But God promised also to sustain, love, and continue with David, and he did so even through the hurricane-like storm of the same chapters. In the end, the enemies are defeated (or pardoned), the kingdom is restored, and the promises remain intact. Sometimes things look bleak for God's people. Sometimes all we can do is hold on to the promises of God. David is not perfect in these chapters, but he does model ongoing trust in God amid awful circumstances (see 15:30; 16:10–21).

A REJECTED KING. We should never be surprised when God's chosen leader (of any era) is reviled and rejected—from Moses and Joshua to David and Solomon and to Jesus, it has been much the same. Opposition is sure for God's son (Ps. 2:1–3), as are the promises that opposition will be futile (Ps. 2:4–12). David faced opposition for two long portions of his life (1 Samuel 18–2 Samuel 4; and 2 Samuel 15–20). The true, final Christ was rejected throughout his entire earthly life: "He came to his own, and his own people did not receive him" (John 1:11). He was hunted in his infancy and plotted against relentlessly until his crucifixion. This is the height of wickedness, but it is also the very plan of God for our salvation (see Acts 2:23; 4:27–28). And Jesus did not remain dead. So now, as followers of Jesus, we can join him "outside the camp and bear the reproach he endured" (Heb. 13:13).

REJECTED, BUT WHY? Jesus and David shared experiences of rejection. However, at least in the case of David's second season of opposition (2 Samuel 15–20), David faced rejection as part of his discipline for sin (12:9–14). The words of the Davidic covenant, "When he commits iniquity, I will discipline him" (7:14), are proven true in 2 Samuel 15–20; in fact, they are proven necessary for every Davidic king after David as well—except one. This is an important contrast between Jesus and every other Davidic king preceding him. Jesus was not disciplined for his own sin, for he was perfectly righteous (Heb. 4:15). Rather, on the cross, Jesus, as a perfect sacrifice, instead bore the weight of *our* iniquity in our place (Heb. 9:15).

Whole-Bible Connections

CHARIOTS. Going back to the exodus, chariots in Scripture are often a symbol for human ingenuity and of *trust in* that human ingenuity. The words of Psalm 20:7 were appropriate to the days of Moses and of David: "Some trust in chariots . . . but we trust in the name of the LORD our God." The same sentiment is behind David's words in his first battle: "The LORD saves not with sword and spear. For the battle is the LORD's" (1 Sam. 17:47)—and chariots could have been added to the list of ways in which the Lord does not save. Therefore, it may have seemed harmless, or even wise, when Absalom "got himself a chariot and horses" (2 Sam. 15:1). But this is a clue carefully placed by the author, foreshadowing the scenes to follow. This marks Absalom's trust in human ingenuity rather than in the Lord. It is reminiscent of Saul, who was always leaning on his spear (1 Sam. 18:10; 19:9; 22:6). The question for us today is this: what chariots, horses, or spears do we lean on in place of the Lord?

KIDRON VALLEY AND MOUNT OF OLIVES. Fleeing their assailants, David and his men made a fateful trek across the Kidron Valley (2 Sam. 15:23) and up the Mount of Olives (v. 30). In the moment, their flight is significant because the rightful king (*God's* king) is fleeing his capital city; the people's weeping (vv. 23, 30) signals its tragic significance. However, it will become further significant when another rejected, Davidic king makes the very same trek. After his time with the disciples in the upper room, Jesus "went out with his disciples across the brook Kidron, where there was a garden" (John 18:1). There, in this garden upon the Mount of Olives, Jesus would be betrayed and arrested. The similarities are surely not coincidental—Jesus was identifying himself with the old rejected king, David, as he retraced his steps. Yet the differences are noteworthy—David was rescued *from* death in the following chapters, while Jesus was rescued *through* death, in his resurrection.

Theological Soundings

DARKNESS OF SIN. All sin is ugly, heinous rebellion against our loving Creator, but this is not to say that all sin is *equally* heinous or willful. We instinctively know this when we are rightfully repulsed by the manifold malevolent sins of 2 Samuel 11–16: adultery, rape, murder, etc. These are stomach-turning matters. Yet, such sins can illuminate powerfully the essence of sin—of any sin. Sin is dark; it is a satanic revolt against God and his ways; it harms others; it is self-destructive; it pulls us deeper in and further down like a vortex. There are no little or petty sins. Prayerfully ponder with the psalmist: "If you, O LORD, should mark iniquities, O Lord, who could stand? But with you there is forgiveness, that you may be feared" (Ps. 130:3–4).

Personal Implications

Take time to reflect on the implications of 2 Samuel 15–20 for your own life today. Consider what you have learned that might lead you to praise God, repent of sin, and trust more deeply in his gracious promises. Write down your reflections under the three headings we have considered and on the passage as a whole.

1. Gospel Glimpses

2. Whole-Bible Connections

3. Theological Soundings

4. 2 Samuel 15–20

As You Finish This Unit . . .

Take a moment now to ask for the Lord's blessing and help as you continue in this study of 1–2 Samuel. And take a moment also to look back through this unit of study, to reflect on some key things that the Lord may be teaching you.

Definition

[1] **Kingdom of God** – The sovereign rule of God. At the present time, the fallen, sinful world does not submit to the kingdom of God, since it does not heed God's rule. Instead, God's kingdom is manifest most clearly in heaven and among his people (Matt. 6:9–10; Luke 17:20–21). After Christ returns, however, the kingdoms of the world will fully submit to the kingdom of God (Rev. 11:15). All people will, either willingly or regretfully, acknowledge his sovereignty (Phil. 2:9–11). Even the natural world will be included in this eternal kingdom (Rom. 8:19–23).

WEEK 11: SUMMARY SNAPSHOTS OF THE DAVIDIC KINGDOM

2 Samuel 21–24

▲

This final section of 1–2 Samuel provides a conclusion to the two books, not by recounting David's final days (for that, see 1 Kings 1–2) but by recording six summary snapshots taken from various seasons of David's life. On the whole, these snapshots paint a portrait of David as a king who is flawed but continues to demonstrate repentance and trust in the Lord; therefore, he is used by God to lead Israel out of trouble and into worship. Of primary importance to this section is the fulfillment of God's promises to sustain his anointed and to defeat his people's enemies (see 1 Sam. 2:1–10).

The Big Picture

God fulfills his promises for a king who will lead and rescue God's people; however, David is a flawed and physically failing king, so God's people must await another, better king.

> ### Reflection and Discussion

Read through the complete passage for this study, 2 Samuel 21–24. Then review the questions below concerning this section of 1–2 Samuel and write your notes on them. (For further background, see the *ESV Study Bible*, pages 576–584; available online at esv.org.)

The last four chapters of 1–2 Samuel form an epilogue. Its six sections are assembled in a chiastic structure—the first relating to the last, the second relating to the fifth, and the third and fourth relating to each other:

> A king's sin brings catastrophe; David intervenes (21:1–14)
>> David's mighty men in action (21:15–22)
>>> David's poetic reflection on deliverance (22:1–51)
>>> David's poetic "last words" (23:1–7)
>> David's mighty men by name (23:9–39)
> A king's sin brings catastrophe; David repents (24:1–25)

Observe this structure for yourself, noting any other similarities you see in the corresponding pairs of passages.

Having observed this literary structure, we will examine the corresponding pairs of texts together.

1. Two Famines (21:1–14; 24:1–25)

We have no other record of Saul's attempting to eradicate the Gibeonites (21:2), but we do find biblical background explaining why Saul's intentions were so serious and sinful. Read Joshua 9:3–21 and discuss how that passage illuminates the seriousness of Saul's actions.

While some aspects of the first famine story (2 Sam. 21:1–14) may seem surprising or strange, what broader theological issues might they illustrate?

The taking of a census (a counting of population) was not always sinful—indeed, Numbers is a whole book about numbering God's people! But David's census is clearly sinful (24:10), although we are not explicitly told why. Based on a recurring theme in the book (see 1 Sam. 2:9–10; 10:23–24; 14:6; 16:7; 17:4–11, 45, 47), why do you think David's census is sinful?

While 2 Samuel 24 ends on the happy note of David's intercession and the Lord's mercy (vv. 18–25), something even more significant is happening. Read 1 Chronicles 21:28–22:1, which retells the same scene with more detail. What is the significance of this moment for the broader plan of God?

---

2. Two Accounts of the Mighty Men (21:15–22; 23:9–39)

Having already read of David's defeat of Goliath in 1 Samuel 17, we might think that 2 Samuel 21:19 is in error when it claims that Elhanan killed Goliath. But this is no contradiction if Goliath was a family name or nickname (see *ESV Study Bible* note on 2 Sam. 21:19). However, we should consider the relationship between the two Philistine wars from another angle. Who was unwilling to fight in 1 Samuel 17? Who is willing to fight in 2 Samuel 21? What does this say about the state of the army before and after David's reign?

When the Philistine warriors are described (21:15–22), what is emphasized? How might this emphasis relate to previous narratives and general themes of 1–2 Samuel?

How does your answer to the above relate to the descriptions of David's mighty men in 2 Samuel 21:15–22 and 23:8–39?

The accounts of David's mighty men include both positive and negative elements. This signifies that, on the whole, David's kingdom includes both weaknesses and strengths. What are they? (Note especially 21:15–17 and 23:11.)

----

3. Two Concluding Poems (22:1–51; 23:1–7)

In a chiastic structure, the middle section is often of central importance. In this case, the middle section is the poetry of 22:1–51 and 23:1–7. In light of the narratives on either side, how does the poetry stand out? How do David's prayers compare and contrast with the scenes before and after?

Recall from earlier in our study how Hannah's prayer (1 Sam. 2:1–10) foreshadows many themes in the rest of 1–2 Samuel and how David's concluding prayer (22:1–51) uses similar language. Note again the similarities, especially in the beginning and the ending of the two bookending prayers.

What differences do you see in the two prayers (see especially 1 Sam. 2:9–10 and 2 Sam. 22:47–51)? In other words, what has changed from the beginning to the end of 1–2 Samuel?

David celebrates God's many acts of deliverance in his concluding prayer (22:1–51). Recall and write down some of the deliverance stories from earlier in 1–2 Samuel that he likely has in mind.

Consider any one of the deliverance stories you recalled above—how does David's celebration of deliverance in 2 Samuel 22:1–51 differ from the actual event? What is noteworthy about the language David uses in his praise?

Read through the following three sections on *Gospel Glimpses, Whole-Bible Connections*, and *Theological Soundings*. Then take time to consider the *Personal Implications* these sections may have for you.

Gospel Glimpses

SIN, WRATH, AND SUBSTITUTION.[1] The famine of 2 Samuel 21 is difficult on a number of levels, but on each point a gospel-related truth is being illustrated. Consider four difficulties and what they illustrate. (1) Saul's sin of murdering Gibeonites results in a nationwide judgment from God. This may seem unfair to the average Israelite, but we should be familiar with the idea of a federal representative; for instance, consider Adam, whose sin led humanity into sin and judgment (Rom. 5:12). And, as we have seen many times in 1–2 Samuel, *as it goes with the king, so it goes for the people.* (2) It may seem a small matter that Saul broke an old promise made with foreigners, but Joshua 9 makes clear that this was a covenant made in God's name, and it would violate his name to break this covenant. God is a holy God who is jealous for his name and takes sin seriously. (3) The solution to the famine—seven sons of Saul being hanged (2 Sam. 21:6)—does not seem like a proper solution. Indeed, Scripture makes clear that sons are not to be punished for the sins of their fathers (Deut. 24:16; Ezek. 18:20). David seems to be doing what he thinks is right, but in so doing he demonstrates both his flawed understanding of justice and also the need for a later, greater king to mete out justice perfectly. Such is what Jesus accomplished on the cross. And yet, let us not miss that God mercifully honored David's prayer (2 Sam. 21:14), despite his flawed attempt at justice. (4) If the scene on top of that Gibeon mountain seems unnecessarily gruesome, we should remember the gruesome scene on top of Mount Golgotha (John 19:17). The Bible is, in fact, full of blood—the problem of sin is that great, and so the payment needed is incredibly severe. But, praise God, Jesus *has* paid the debt and removed God's judgment for all who believe and ask for his mercy (see Heb. 9:11–15, 23–28).

Whole-Bible Connections

THRESHING FLOOR, TEMPLE, AND BEYOND. The prophet Gad directs David exactly where to go and what to do: "Raise an altar to the LORD on the threshing floor of Araunah the Jebusite" (2 Sam. 24:18). And so David does, and so 2 Samuel ends. However, the book of 1 Chronicles tells the same story with an important added detail: "Then David said, '*Here shall be the house of the LORD God*'" (1 Chron. 22:1). Consider the significance of this moment in light of earlier and later seasons of God's plan. Recall the early days of the tabernacle,[2] where God dwelt in the midst of his sojourning people. Soon God began to talk of a "place" to which he would lead them, a place of more permanent worship (Deut. 12:5–6). We finally discover the name of that place in 2 Samuel 5: Jerusalem. The anticipation swells when David brings the ark of the covenant (the symbol of God's presence) into Jerusalem (2 Samuel 6), and even more when David talks of building a permanent dwelling for God (7:2). Of course, God's alternate plan (7:5–16) is hardly discouraging—David's son will build this house for God (a temple[3]), and God will build for David an eternal house (offspring). Second Samuel ends on the very precipice of these promises being realized: the threshing floor of Araunah is ground zero for the glorious dwelling of God in the midst of his people (see 1 Kings 8–9). And yet, the promises do not end there; the roller-coaster ride of God's plan does not stop with the completion of Solomon's temple (1 Kings 10–11). Not long after, the kingdom is irreparably split in two (1 Kings 12). Later, the grand temple is destroyed, and God's people are taken away. A generation later, God's people return and rebuild out of the ruins, but the new temple is only a glimmer of its former glory (Ezra 3:12). Anticipation and tension are raised in equal measure when the prophets foresee a supernatural temple of global glory and blessing (Ezekiel 40–48). All of these streams of promise, anticipation, and tension come together when Jesus explains that he is the true temple (Matt. 12:6; John 1:14; 2:19; Heb. 10:20), and that by his Spirit he will dwell in his people forever (John 14:15–23; Rev. 21:3).

Theological Soundings

ENEMIES CONQUERED. David rightly lamented, "How many are my foes!" (Ps. 3:1), but in the end he rightly praises God for deliverance from all of his enemies (2 Sam. 22:1). Yet, there are greater enemies in this world than a Saul, an Absalom, or a whole Philistine army—as real and great as those threats were.

Satan, sin, guilt, and the sentence of death (both physical and eternal) are much fiercer enemies. In fact, these are the ultimate enemies standing behind a Saul or a Goliath. Therefore, it is of great and lasting comfort to know that Christ has defeated Satan (Heb. 2:14–15), triumphing over all spiritual authorities and putting them to shame (Col. 2:15). He abolished death and brought life (2 Tim. 2:10). All things are now in subjection to him (1 Cor. 15:27). We do not yet see everything in subjection to him, but one day this reality will be clear to all (Heb. 2:8). So even now we can rejoice and give him great praise: the battle is the Lord's and is as good as done.

SEEN AND UNSEEN. David's psalms that reflect upon a specific event (e.g., Pss. 3; 34; 56; 57; 60) often include rich, symbolic imagery describing the enemy's threat and God's help. David's final songs in 2 Samuel (22:1–51; 23:1–7) are no exception. They portray God's answers to David's prayer for help in apocalyptic-like terms: God's cracking open the earth, devouring with fire, riding on a cherub, throwing lightning bolts, and exposing the depths of the sea (22:8–16). David could be accused of hyperbole in light of the actual events in 1–2 Samuel: David threw a stone and Goliath fell; Saul threw a spear and David ducked; David was hungry and the priest gave him bread; David was nabbed in Gath, so he acted crazy and got away. On and on we could go. On one level, these events do not look supernatural, let alone cataclysmic. But on another level, they were. Christians believe there are two realms, the seen and the unseen (see Dan. 10:12–13; Eph. 6:12). Therefore, we can praise God with extravagant language even when answered prayer, protection, and provision appear rather ordinary. Though we may see only the slingshot or spittle (again, see 1 Sam. 21:13), the omnipotent Lord is always at work in glorious, often unseen, ways.

> ## Personal Implications

Take time to reflect on the implications of 2 Samuel 21–24 for your own life today. Consider what you have learned that might lead you to praise God, repent of sin, and trust more deeply in his gracious promises. Write down your reflections under the three headings we have considered and on the passage as a whole.

1. Gospel Glimpses

2. Whole-Bible Connections

3. Theological Soundings

4. 2 Samuel 21–24

As You Finish This Unit . . .

Take a moment now to ask for the Lord's blessing and help as you continue in this study of 1–2 Samuel. And take a moment also to look back through this unit of study, to reflect on some key things that the Lord may be teaching you.

Definitions

[1] **Substitution** – The means by which Jesus' death on the cross took effect: Jesus offered himself to die as a substitute for believers. He took upon himself the punishment they deserve and thereby reconciled them to God.

[2] **Tabernacle** – The tent where God dwelled on earth and communed with his people as Israel's divine King. Also referred to as the "tent of meeting" (Lev. 1:5), the temple in Jerusalem later replaced it.

[3] **Temple** – Solomon built the first temple in Jerusalem, to replace the portable tabernacle. This temple was later destroyed by the Babylonians, rebuilt, enlarged, and then destroyed again by the Romans in AD 70.

Week 12: Summary and Conclusion

▲

We conclude our study by summarizing the big picture of God's message through 1–2 Samuel as a whole. Then we will consider several questions in order to reflect on various *Gospel Glimpses*, *Whole-Bible Connections*, and *Theological Soundings* throughout 1–2 Samuel.

The Big Picture of 1–2 Samuel

The books of Samuel are about Israel's first kings. They anticipate the need for a king (1 Sam. 2:10), portray the wrong kind of king (1 Samuel 8–15), and present the right king (1 Samuel 16ff.), while also making clear that another, better king is still needed. The promises given to David for an eternal, righteous throne (2 Samuel 7) are too big for David to fulfill. He is a flawed and finite king. Only a perfect and eternal son of David can fulfill what David rightly interprets as a "charter for mankind" (7:19). Jesus is that Son of David, and "all the promises of God find their Yes in him" (2 Cor. 1:20). He is "King of kings and Lord of lords," and at his name "every knee [will] bow . . . and every tongue confess that Jesus Christ is Lord" (Rev. 19:16; Phil. 2:10–11).

The stories of 1–2 Samuel are not first and foremost moral examples for us to imitate or shun. Rather, these narratives primarily teach us about our need for a righteous ruler, a rescuer, a warrior king who will crush the enemy for good. They teach us about God's faithfulness to provide righteousness and peace through his Son (see Psalm 2), in God's own timing and way. Studying 1–2 Samuel should produce thankfulness to God that the true Son has come and a perfect kingdom has been ushered in (Matt. 4:17). This should lead us to submit ourselves to this good King, represent him well to the world, and continue to pray "your kingdom come" as we await the final day when the kingdoms of this world become the kingdom of Christ (Rev. 11:15).

The narratives of 1–2 Samuel do, however, secondarily provide examples that should either inspire or warn us (see Rom. 15:4; 1 Cor. 10:6, 11 for this use of the Old Testament). At times, David is an incredible example of courage, kindness, worship, and/or humility—how can we not be instructed and inspired! At other times, he or others (especially Saul) provide a warning regarding the power of temptation and the ugliness of sin.

Gospel Glimpses

As we have seen, 1–2 Samuel is rich with developments in God's glorious plan to save sinners and bring forth his kingdom, often in surprising and seemingly upside-down ways, particularly through his anointed, who in the eyes of the world does not look like a strong king. We gain a glimpse of this in King David, but the substance and fulfillment of this truth comes roughly a thousand years later in Jesus Christ, the true Son of God and final King.

How has 1–2 Samuel helped you to see your sin and your need for a Savior?

How has 1–2 Samuel brought new clarity to your understanding of the gospel?

What particular passages or themes in 1–2 Samuel have led you to a fresh understanding and grasp of God's grace to us through Jesus?

> ## Whole-Bible Connections

A proper study of 1–2 Samuel requires attention to God's broader plan of redemption, to promises that precede 1–2 Samuel (especially the promises given to Abraham in Genesis 12; 15; and 17), and to developments that follow the time of David (such as the temple, the prophets, and the whole New Testament era). In short, exploring 1–2 Samuel leads us all over the Bible. The books are a window into an epoch of history in which promises of old are beginning to come to pass and new promises are made, while many promises still await fulfillment as we leave David on the threshing floor of Araunah in 2 Samuel 24.

How has this study of 1–2 Samuel amplified your understanding of the biblical storyline of redemption?

What themes emphasized in 1–2 Samuel have helped you to deepen your grasp of the Bible's unity?

What passages or themes have expanded your understanding of the redemption that Jesus provides, which he began at his first coming and will consummate at his return?

What connections between 1–2 Samuel and the New Testament were new to you? What connections between David and Jesus have you learned of?

Theological Soundings

The books of 1–2 Samuel do not necessarily offer unique contributions to Christian theology, but many theological themes are clarified and/or demonstrated, often in vivid color, such as the nature of sin and the character of God.

Has your theology shifted in any minor or major ways during the course of studying 1–2 Samuel? How so?

How has your understanding of the nature and character of God been deepened through this study?

What unique contributions does 1–2 Samuel make toward our understanding of who Jesus is and what he accomplished through his life, death, and resurrection?

What does 1–2 Samuel teach us about the human condition and our need of redemption?

Personal Implications

God wrote 1–2 Samuel to transform you. As you reflect on 1–2 Samuel as a whole, what implications do you see for your own life?

What implications for life flow from your reflections on the questions already asked in this week's study concerning *Gospel Glimpses*, *Whole-Bible Connections*, and *Theological Soundings*?

What have you learned in 1–2 Samuel that might lead you to praise God, turn away from sin, or trust more firmly in his promises?

▶ As You Finish Studying 1–2 Samuel . . .

We rejoice with you as you finish this study of 1–2 Samuel! May this study become part of your Christian walk of faith, day by day and week by week throughout all your life. We would greatly encourage you to study the Word of God on a week-by-week basis. To continue your study of the Bible, we would encourage you to consider other books in the Knowing the Bible series and to visit knowingthebibleseries.org.

Lastly, take a moment to look back through this study. Review the notes that you have written and the things that you have highlighted or underlined. Reflect again on the key themes that the Lord has been teaching you about himself and about his Word. We pray that these truths and lessons will become a treasure for the rest of your life, in the name of the Father, and the Son, and the Holy Spirit. Amen.